Coming Home to Who You Are

Coming Home
to Who You Are

Discovering Your Natural Capacity
for Love, Integrity, and Compassion

DAVID RICHO

SHAMBHALA
Boston & London
2012

Shambhala Publications, Inc.
Horticultural Hall
300 Massachusetts Avenue
Boston, Massachusetts 02115
www.shambhala.com

© 2008, 2012 David Richo

Completely revised and expanded edition of *Everyday Commitments:
Choosing a Life of Love, Realism, and Acceptance* (Shambhala, 2008).

9 8 7 6 5 4 3 2 1

First Edition
Printed in the United States of America

♾ This edition is printed on acid-free paper that meets
the American National Standards Institute z39.48 Standard.
♻ This book is printed on 30% postconsumer recycled paper.
For more information please visit www.shambhala.com.

Distributed in the United States by Random House, Inc.,
and in Canada by Random House of Canada Ltd

Designed by James D. Skatges

Library of Congress Cataloging-in-Publication Data
Richo, David, 1940–
Coming home to who you are: discovering your natural capacity
for love, integrity, and compassion / David Richo.
p. cm.
Rev. ed. of: Everyday commitments. ©2008.
ISBN 978-1-59030-684-0 (pbk.: alk. paper)
1. Life. 2. Attitude (Psychology) 3. Success. 4. Spirituality.
I. Richo, David, 1940– Everyday commitments. II. Title.
BD431.R525 2012
170'.44—dc23
2011024986

To each
of my students and clients over the years,
with love, respect, and thanks.

So much of what I know
I learned from you.
We all have let the light
Come in and through.

Contents

PART THREE: Becoming As Real As We Can Be

PART FOUR: Being with Others

PART FIVE: Advancing in the Art of Intimacy

Preface

To turn all that we possess into the channel of universal love becomes the business of our lives.

— JOHN WOOLMAN, *The Journal of John Woolman, Quaker*

WHAT DOES IT TAKE to be a really good person? This question has intrigued and challenged me for many years. The answers that began to emerge for me became, in 1998, a list of specific commitments we can all make to a life of integrity and loving-kindness.

Over the years, I continually asked clients, students, and participants in twelve-step programs for feedback that would help me revise my list of commitments. Did they make sense? Did they seem appropriate? Were any of them too much or too little to ask? I made changes in accordance with their suggestions, adding new commitments and revising others. I also became more aware of what I most admired in other people, and added their qualities to my list. I did not include anything that I myself was not willing to put into practice.

These commitments appeared in my books here and there, but they were the central focus of my book *Everyday Commitments*, published in 2008. This new edition is a thoroughly revised and expanded presentation of these essential commitments, including many new realizations that I feel fortunate to have gained over these recent years.

None of the topics I have written about have been so compelling, captivating, and vital to me as these commitments to integrity and loving-kindness. Sharing and living them has become a major purpose—and joy—in my recent life as a therapist, teacher, writer, and practitioner.

What I personally noticed when I chose to live in accord with principles of integrity and loving-kindness was that I liked myself more. That positive feeling about myself encouraged me to persevere in this way of living. But my original motivation was simply a sense of "rightness," not entirely in the moral sense, but rather in the sense of what seems best for a human to be and what so many admirable teachers throughout the ages have recommended.

I am hoping that this book will offer effective technologies that can usher us all into a new way of being alive—as cheerful agents of the goodness that is intrinsically in us all. Every choice we make for integrity and loving-kindness reflects that goodness. Every commitment we keep helps us cocreate a world of justice, peace, and love.

Indeed, the "you" in the title of this book does not refer only to you the reader as an individual. It is you in the collective of humanity. This book is about coming home to who we *all* are and can be; we are bringing *everyone* home to who we all are and can be. All these commitments have one resplendent focus: choosing a life no longer driven by ego, the primacy of "me," but by love, the celebration of "we." Here is our chance for exodus, for a passover from bondage in ego to liberty in love.

Finally, I knew I had progressed in my own practice when it began to make sense to me that these commitments could someday become the style not only of individuals but of institutions and nations. It will require a massive shift away from domination, greed, and exploitation but it can happen. That is the outcome I hope that you, reader-practitioners, will join me in moving toward. It need not be considered a pipe dream for, as Alfred, Lord Tennyson, said in his poem "Ulysses," "'Tis not too late to seek a newer world."

––––––––––––––––––

May we keep coming home to the light of love and wisdom and may we never cease reaching out to those who are still lost in the darkness of fear and craving.

––––––––––––––––––

Introduction

To be human is to be born into the world with something to achieve, namely, the fullness of one's human nature.

—Paul J. Wadell, CP

WHAT A DESTINY IS OURS: our own life story can be a unique depiction of the inherent goodness in all of us. This is a handbook on how we can let that happen wholeheartedly. Here is an owner's guide to being an upright and loving human by committing ourselves to a life of integrity and love. Our motivation is simply the desire to live our lives at the level of the heart.

Our task does not require extensive research. Our inner self knows exactly how to act with integrity and love. As Emma Jung and Marie-Louise von Franz wrote in their book, *The Grail Legend,* "An inner wholeness presses its still unfulfilled claims upon us." Thus, there is already an urge inside us to live in a spiritually mature way. All we have to do is act in accord with it.

According to an article in the *Washington Post,* scientists are discovering that a morally virtuous sense may be physically "hardwired" in us, residing in an area of the brain called the ventromedial prefrontal cortex.* Science also seems to be finding ways to demonstrate that empathy, the foundation of our moral inclinations, flows in our very cells. Perhaps this is why belief in the inherent goodness of humanity appears in so many spiritual traditions. The Roman Stoic philosopher Seneca noticed the way practicing goodness leads to its becoming spontaneous, automatic behavior: "My goodness now requires no thought but has become habit and I cannot act but rightly"—another sign that virtue was in us all along.

In the Buddhist tradition, and in others, "right conduct" is a primary pathway to happiness and enlightened living. We might say it is advanced spiritual etiquette in a world that so often presents us with greed, hatred, and ignorance. In psychological terms, virtuous living leads us to fearless love, freedom from ego-centeredness, and contentment with ourselves and our predicaments.

---

* Shankar Vedantam, "If It Feels Good to Be Good, It Might Be Only Natural," *Washington Post,* May 28, 2007.

In my work over the years as a therapist, and in my own life experience, I have indeed noticed that the healthier people become psychologically, the more goodness they show and the more ethical their choices. (This also works in reverse.) We can dedicate ourselves to practices of integrity and love and soon notice ourselves becoming more psychologically healthy in our decisions, relationships, and behavior. Our behavior is no longer based on childhood conditioning or on primitive attitudes but on our now more evolved spiritual consciousness. We have made the transition from habit to choice—a definition of freedom.

Our commitments cannot be strategies by which we seek to manipulate others into responding kindly or generously to us. Our dedication is not based on others' behavior. We choose to be loving no matter what others do. The Golden Rule is unilateral. It does not promise nor is it conditional upon reciprocity.

At the same time, we might notice that our loving-kindness *can* sometimes turn the ill-will of others into goodwill—"a consummation devoutly to be wished," as Hamlet observed.

We have no way of guaranteeing that anyone will treat us with integrity and loving-kindness. But nothing can stop us from giving our personal guarantee that we will act with integrity and loving-kindness toward everyone. That becomes such a source of joy that we settle more easily into the world just as it is. Loving-kindness is a direct path to the unconditional yes—the courageous stance of opening to whatever arises in our lives, of not shutting down in the face of life's challenges.

Personally, I still believe, even after all the grim events of our recent history, that we humans can trust that we are inherently pure goodness, consciousness, and bliss. They reside, and are always able to arise, in every one of us. They never go away, nor can they be lost in the dark.

We do not have to search for all this light; we must only keep making choices for uprightness and love. Soon we will be deeply feeling—and gladly sharing—the good news that light is our true nature and that love is how we show it. Virginia Woolf, in her novel *The Waves*, shows us what will soon wonderfully happen: "Things are losing their hardness; now even my body lets the light through." What more would we ever want?

> I think it not improbable that a human, like the grub that prepares a chamber for the winged thing it never has seen but is to be—that a human may have cosmic destinies that he does not understand.
>
> —OLIVER WENDELL HOLMES, "Law and the Court," a speech to the Harvard Law School Association of New York, 1913

HOW TO USE THIS BOOK

The chapters that follow offer a program of personal ful-fillment through commitments to integrity and loving-kindness.

Personal fulfillment happens when we are satisfied in three areas: We live in accord with our values, activate our potential, and take the actions that lead to achieving our goals. Our goals are based on our bliss and our talents. Since we contain an innate and ineradicable love, wisdom, and healing power, we are fulfilled and contented when we activate these remarkable gifts. This is coming home to who we are. Discontent can be read as a support-ive signal from our psyche reminding us that we are not home yet and nudging us in that direction.

Commitments are dedications to design our behavior to fulfill our goals.

Integrity means principled and steadfast adherence to standards of honesty, truthfulness, fairness, and trustwor-thiness.

Loving-kindness means aspiring for and acting with caring and compassionate love toward others, near and dear, far and wide.

The program offered in this book invites us into a spir-itual venture. *Spiritual* is that which is both transcendent and immanent. It is transcendent in that it goes beyond the minimum, the usual, the expected, the ordinary realms of consciousness. For example, the minimum definition of *generosity* is "giving." When our giving becomes selfless liberality, it is a spiritual virtue. Caring about others is *love*; when our caring goes the extra mile and becomes self-sacrificing it has spiritual significance.

"Spiritual" is also that which activates the depth of goodness within us—the immanent. Thus, love becomes spiritual when it is unconditional in its expression and universal in its extent. Building a healthy ego is psychological strength. Letting go of a self-centered ego for the sake of love and intimacy is a spiritual victory.

The commitments and practices that follow also present us with tools for self-assessment. We may find ourselves facing questions like these: To what extent do wholesomeness and love characterize my present behavior and attitudes? How committed am I to my psychological work and spiritual practice? How deep is my trust in my own goodness? How willing am I to put myself on the line to show my full dedication to a life of love?

The commitments are not meant to be "shoulds" or moral directives but gentle invitations that stir and steer us to new possibilities in our way of living. They are challenges, guidelines, and opportunities, not demands or obligations. They are concrete dedications to evolving as fully realized humans. To "dedicate" is to place an intention that directs our actions and choices to a specific cause. The heart's cause is a continuity of commitment to integrity and loving-kindness. Why else do we have this lifetime?

The commitments and practices that follow may be inspiring but also intimidating. Very few of us can achieve all these ideals. Nonetheless, we can set our bar high, and then make some strides and perhaps some leaps.

There may be times when we may not remain faithful to our practices; at times we may slack off or procrastinate. Success with these commitments lies not in perfect compliance but in frequent start-overs, ever-new approximations. We are always working with a beginner's mind. Hence, all that matters is that we get under way one more time than we give up, pick up the ball one more time than we drop it, go back to the drawing board one more time than we abandon it. It is never too late to begin nor to come back to practicing—yet another reason to be optimistic about ourselves. Any advance at all can liberate us from fear-based choices in favor of a loving way of living and a healthy way of loving. There is no way to fail except by giving up in despair.

We all have a shadow side. We all have inclinations toward both good and evil, right and wrong, love and hate. What makes us good people has nothing to do with the fact that we have these common human tendencies. What makes us good is that we keep choosing to act on our goodness, rightness, and love most of the time and that when we don't, we make amends. Our continual choices for the light, not our dark potentials, make us who we are. To come home to our true nature is not to have no shadow side to our personality. It is to walk through that dark valley in ourselves without stopping. We can do this without fear of the dark because of our commitment to keep practicing integrity and loving-kindness.

The word *practicing* may lead us to two misleading inferences:

The first is that virtue is only about performing certain acts. Actually, the focus of this book is on virtue-ethics. This is virtuous living by an *overall* dedication to live in accord with our enlightened nature of wisdom, compassion, integrity, love. We are pledging our allegiance to a life of goodness over self-gratification, and of communal values over self-satisfaction. That fundamental life option is what counts. It cannot be accomplished by any single good deed or canceled by any single misdeed.

The second false impression that can follow from our accent on practices is that our spiritual growth is based entirely on our own diligence and perseverance, as if transformation were entirely up to us. But as interconnected beings we are continually supported by others and by powers beyond ego. Our effort works best, in fact, with an acknowledgment of the necessary grace that is ever supporting and upholding our exertions. We do not have to believe in God to see the power of grace. The universe has an uninterrupted evolutionary direction. When we are aligned to the work of cocreating a world of loving-kindness, that evolutionary direction becomes personal in us. This can feel like—be recognized as the equivalent of—a transcendent force working through us. It is a higher power than our ego and it can feel like a presence that is an assisting force on our life journey. That evolutionary force, always reliable not always visible, is "grace." It hearkens to us from beyond ego and, in that sense, is transcendent.

The force of grace may lead us to reorient our motivations and goals in life. We can revise our set of values. Our values are defined by those principles that matter most to us and that direct our choices and behavior. We can begin to care about awakening more than achieving, selflessness more than ego-aggrandizement, wanting all beings to be free from fear and craving rather than being concerned only with our own liberation. This turning in a new direction is called *bodhicitta* in Buddhism. We become aware of—and choose to act in accord with—a deeply spiritual potential in ourselves, that which is called "buddha nature," the life inside us, beyond ego, that which is permanent, blissful, and unconditioned by greed, hatred, or ignorance.

Though anyone can become enlightened, in my view, the bodhicitta moment comes to us as a grace, so we cannot conjure it by effort or willpower alone. Grace is beyond cause and effect. But we can place ourselves in the best position for that awakening and reorienting to happen. That "best position" is our pure intention to act in accord with our enlightened nature. Our dedication to the commitments and practices in the following chapters is thus coming home to who we really are in our full and radiant aliveness—the apogee of humanness.

Each practice in this book offers us a resource, one that perhaps until now has gone unnoticed. We gather, practice by practice, a collection of inner resources, interior assets, and skillful means we can turn to for comfort and strength in troubled times. Gradually, the excitement we feel in having found trustworthy resources and in dedicating ourselves to integrity and love becomes more valuable than material gain, prestige, popularity, or whether people like or want us. This new criterion for what matters is the best benefit this book can offer.

In approaching our practices, we can distinguish willpower from willingness. "Willpower" combines effortful intention and fervent goal-seeking. "Willingness" is placing an intention, and that automatically moves us toward our goal. In this book we work by willingness, open to the release of our natural capacity for love, integrity, and compassion. We are not pushing ourselves toward an objective but opening ourselves so that our wholeness can unfold. That is how our life purpose and our psychological-spiritual practice become one and the same.

The commitments in this book may at times seem "over the top" in what they ask of us. But they are meant for nothing less than a whole new set of motivations, a new lifestyle, a new way of being human. Hopefully, our standards will transcend those of the majority of society. For instance, we have been taught to get back at people who offend us. Our new lifestyle does not include re-venge. Instead we speak up, refuse to allow further abuse, and hope that the offender may be transformed into a more loving person. Our commitment to nonretaliation shows that we now believe in reparability and the inherent goodness of everyone. "Getting our licks in" is also no longer one of our goals because we have become spiritually oriented and lovingly motivated, not ego-centered. This includes not gloating over the sufferings or defeats of those who have hurt us. "What goes around comes around" becomes "May what goes around come around *transformatively*." Thus, a reversal of attitude and belief happens in us when love has triumphed in our hearts. It happened to a seventh-century Orthodox monk, Saint Isaac of Syria, who then wrote: "God's response to sinners is not what we consider just punishment, but the reward of resurrection."

We see the same generous spirit in the eighth-century Buddhist teacher, Shantideva:

> May those whose hell it is to hate and hurt
> Be turned into lovers bringing flowers.

Here are some specific suggestions for working with this book so that you can get the most out of it:

- Before contemplating a commitment, take a few deep breaths and notice how you feel physically. Make an intention and look for ways to bring your body, with its senses and movements, into each practice. Mindfulness meditation, described below, will also be a useful way to begin and conclude each chapter.

• You may want to use the following three-part exercise every day or once a week: (1) Read and reflect on a single chapter; (2) visualize yourself acting in accord with that commitment; (3) look for ways throughout the day or week to design your behavior accordingly—this means being on the lookout for practical and specific ways to implement these ideals beyond what the book suggests.

• When you finish reading a chapter, read aloud the commitment that appears at the end of it. Write it out and place it where it will be a visible reminder to you throughout the day or week. It can serve as an affirmation, aspiration, or intention.

• Make an audio recording of the commitments (those in the body of the book or the shorter list that appears in the appendix) so you can listen to them in your own voice from time to time. Hearing yourself stating the commitments reinforces them as dedications you are taking seriously.

• Use the statements at the end of each chapter, or those in the appendix, as a checklist for reflecting on the ethical choices you have faced in the past and those that might be facing you now. Look upon your past decisions with compassionate understanding and without regret or self-blame. All that matters now is your choice for healthy behavior in the future.

- Ask someone you trust for feedback on how (or whether) your behavior reflects the specific ideals you are working on.

- The commitments in this book can be useful for people in twelve-step programs who are taking an inventory of their behavior. (This was the purpose I first envisioned when I began to compile the commitments.)

- Couples can work with this book jointly. All the practices together describe intimacy-promoting behavior and authentic commitment. The practices can be contemplated as an auditing tool to examine the "state of the union." They can also become promises one or both partners make to the other to establish, or rebuild basic trust.

- The commitments can serve as criteria for choosing a suitable partner. Choosing or staying with a partner who does not act with integrity and loving-kindness also makes you question what you yourself are up to. Are you looking for happiness and a good life or have you become attached to someone who feels good in some way but may not be good to or for you?

- Write a poem or journal entry in response to a commitment and notice what new information may come through to you.

- Practices gain power as we attend to simultaneous messages that may be arising from our unconscious. While working with this book, pay close attention to dreams and synchronicity, meaningful coincidence, to see if they reflect themes that are similar to those in the practices. This is how the universe, or higher power, may be joining in on your evolutionary changes. That joining is another form of grace.

- As you continue in your practices, or at any time, you may want to say this: "Though I am not always successful in virtuous living or in keeping my commitments, these are the ideals I am placing an intention to live by. I am not hard on myself when I fail to live up to these ideals. What matters is that I keep trying. I am not perfect, but I am sincerely committed to working on myself." You may want to add these words of the Dalai Lama: "The purity of my intention is my protection."

PRACTICING MINDFULNESS

As noted above, it is helpful to begin and end the practices in this book with mindfulness meditation. Find a place where you can sit quietly, free of distractions, and focus on your breath. Simply notice your breathing in and breathing out.

Let thoughts pass through your mind without holding on to them or rejecting them. Let go of the judgments, comparisons, and fantasies that embroider your thoughts. Silently acknowledge and label each activity of your mind as "thought" and keep returning to awareness of your breath. When you do this, you decrease the power your thoughts have over you and increase your own power to be the imperturbable witness of your experience.

The reason we keep returning to our breath is because it can only happen in the present. Hence our breath resettles and anchors us in the here and now. We are no longer fleeing to the past or future, which can distract or destabilize us.

Placing our attention on our breath alone and not engaging with our thoughts and feelings may seem unnatural. This may be because such behaviors are antithetical to how we originally survived as humans. In prehistoric times, we could not afford to concentrate on any one thing for very long nor to disregard any clues from the environment or intuitions from within ourselves. After all, a saber-toothed tiger might be waiting for an off-guard moment. Mindfulness is radically contemporary, securely settling us in the present.

When you move from thought to breath, you are like the mother who sees her baby rhythmically banging a knife on the table. She gently removes the knife and with a smile begins clapping his hands together playing patty-cake in his same rhythm. Focusing on our breath is the equivalent of this nurturant redirection, a pleasurable alternative to our dangerously distracting thoughts. The mother is not angry or panicked as she redirects her baby's focus from the knife to the clapping. She smiles and uses a kindly tone of voice as she does so. This is the voice with which you label your thoughts, including a smile each time. Such placid and patient warmth is a form of loving-kindness to yourself. In fact, mindfulness can be a lead-in to the loving-kindness practice described in the following section.

Mindfulness is not just something we do once a day as part of our attempts at self-improvement. It is a spiritual practice of relating to people and experiences in daily life too. At any time throughout the day, you can notice your thoughts, feelings, sensations, and reactions without having to be caught up in the story lines that surround them, for example, judgment, fear, control, and so forth. Now you are experiencing bare attention, an awareness no longer cloaked in your usual thoughts and projections. You are observing your feelings and experiences as a noncensoring witness who keeps coming back to the bare-bones reality of what is going on in the naked moment.

Mindfulness means experiencing without reference to your own story, needs, wishes, beliefs, assumptions, ego-centeredness. This puts you in contact with your true self beyond any conditioning or conditions. Only what is observed from the vantage point of that self is seen rightly.

You are now able to witness even your inclinations and impulses without feeling compelled to gratify them. They lose their power to draw or repel you, so you can make a choice rather than have to act on a compulsion. You have found an evenness and imperturbability in the face of any experience or happening. With this equanimity you are not so ignited as to be anxious nor so numb as to be nonresponsive. You do not deny your feelings but instead let them pass through you in their full arc and go to ground. Indeed, you can remain grounded in all emotional weathers. Practicing mindful equanimity is a skillful means toward grounding yourself. You are no longer at the mercy of attachment or repulsion—our oh-so-short egoic repertory of reactions to what happens to us.

Now you feel safe and secure in yourself in the moment because you have become a person with options. You are no longer forced to attach to something because of attraction, nor recoil from anything because of aversion. You are protected from the greed that can result from grasping for what attracts you and the hatred that can result from turning against what repels you. Attraction and repulsion are natural, but compulsive ways of reacting to them can cause suffering or lead to unwise actions.

Whether you approach or avoid experiences is now a conscious choice not a conditioned reaction, making it possible for you to regulate them rather than be controlled by them (or become controlling because of them). You become adept at living courageously in your present reality and showing love to others fearlessly. In both there are now no holds barred, no limits imposed, no ventures prohibited—and most of all, no secret lairs where the ego can take cover.

Once our ego is no longer in the way, our thoughts and feelings can drop down directly into the depth of our true self. When we arrive at this real home of ourselves, we come upon all our human riches: Our potential is already and always fully realized. Our knowledge and skills are in perfect attunement. Our equanimity is unassailable. Our psychological-spiritual integration is complete. Our goodness and our love of others is unconditional. Our lights and shadows rest side by side as lambs of serenity and lions of strength.

As we continue to join our equanimity to mindfulness meditation, we feel this egoless depth in ourselves as the homestead of contemplation, a snug inner silence. We firmly trust that it—we—can now hold and provide a safe landing for any circumstance or predicament. We no longer have to go to the people, places, and compulsions that failed us in the past. They were never really refuges, only the hiding places of ego after all.

This practice helps us learn to reduce our stress levels. We no longer are so apt to absorb and hold on to pain but instead we let it flow through us. We want to avoid the

Scylla and Charybdis, the extremes, where either we react so much that we are flooded or we react so little that everything becomes like water off a duck's back.

Buddhism radically differs from many other approaches to spirituality in that the way, the path of wisdom and serenity, is not beyond us but within us. Our comfort and strength are not found sometime in the future, somewhere other than here, in some new situation, or once we are someone else. The present moment, in this place, in this predicament, just as we are, *is* the path. Mindfulness is the practice that keeps bringing us home to this amazing grace.

> The practice of meditation is not so much about the hypothetical attainment of enlightenment. It is about leading a good life.
>
> —CHÖGYAM TRUNGPA, *Smile at Fear*

CULTIVATING LOVING-KINDNESS

According to Buddhist tradition, we are all endowed with four ineradicable and limitless capacities: love, compassion, joy at others' happiness, and equanimity. The loving-kindness (*metta*) practice helps us cultivate these gifts for ourselves and for everyone else. It calls upon our imagination to combine aspiration, intention, and behavior.

We begin by briefly centering ourselves in mindfulness. We sit quietly and *aspire* to feel, *intend*, and *show* the four capacities of our and everyone's true nature: love, compassion, joy, and equanimity. Mindfulness leads to loving-kindness, since we can focus on our basic, inherent, unconditional goodness without interfering ego mindsets—what we bring to what we see, our expectations, beliefs, judgments, projections. Loving-kindness leads back to mindfulness, since we are bringing bare attention to our practice, this time the attention of love without conditions or reservations.

To love is to want those we love to be happy. We say aloud or silently, "May I experience happiness." Then we extend this same happiness to those we love, saying, "May [name of person we love] experience happiness." Next, we extend the wish for happiness to those toward whom we are indifferent, then to those with whom we are having difficulties, then finally to all beings. The cycle is repeated, focusing on each of our capacities, one at a time. We can alter the phrases or order, as long as we express heartfelt care both for ourselves and others.

Many of us were brought up to believe that it is selfish to focus on our own happiness, especially in this way where we intentionally wish it for ourselves first. But in the loving-kindness practice we are not selfish but self-caring. Selfishness is concentrating on one's own needs at the expense of or to the exclusion of others', invariably preferring oneself over others. In the loving-kindness practice we specifically include others, and then all others, in the phrases immediately following our reference to ourselves. In addition, love and compassion for oneself *is* the best path to love and compassion for others.

In the Madhyama Agama Sutra 86, Buddha says, "The mind of love . . . increases immeasurably and eventually can embrace the entire world." When we practice loving-kindness each day, our circle of love expands to become all-inclusive and unconditional. In other words, loving-kindness practice helps us fulfill our inner urge toward wholeness. The practice also helps us fulfill our human destiny to create a world of justice, peace, and love. Here we also notice another reason that the capacities of our true nature are called "immeasurable": they automatically reach beyond ourselves to the world. This fits with Aristotle's view that goodness can't help but spread itself around, forever and everywhere.

Buddha even goes so far as to say that the practice of loving-kindness continues after death. In the Anguttara Nikaya Sutta we read that the practitioner of loving-kindness "is reborn in the Brahma heaven where he can continue the practice because he will find a *sangha* [community] of people there practicing the four immeasurables."

Our loving-kindness practice can soften our aggressive impulses so that our inner goodness and inclination toward maintaining connection with others can come to the fore. Loving-kindness practice can help us let go of ego reactivity when we apply our aspirations to situations that might ordinarily arouse us. For instance, when someone cuts us off in traffic, we can take a breath, slow down, and say something like the following: "May you arrive safely at your destination without harming anyone. May you find serenity in courteous driving. May all drivers like you find the practice of loving-kindness." If someone is curt toward us, we might say, under our breath, "May you feel better today. May your benevolence shine through." If a political figure appearing on TV is one who we believe to be inept or erroneous, we can say, "May you support policies that lead to peace. May you grow in wisdom and competence. May you become fully enlightened." Our aspirations for what is traditionally referred to as conversion have no limit, because they are based on our unreserved trust in the essential goodness of humanity and its natural urge to manifest.

Thus, in the loving-kindness practice we are finding out not only what our kindly voice sounds like but also how far our love can extend, how much warmth we can radiate, how much hope we have in the possibility of enlightenment for all beings. This is how we say yes to what is most real in us, our true nature, our immeasurable capacity for trust in humanity's potential for bodhicitta.

Our dedication fully influences our lifestyle: We dedicate ourselves to showing love and compassion to everyone. We are intent on bringing happiness to others, not pain. We are happy about others' success. We want peace everywhere and in everyone. We respond to others with equanimity rather than retort with aggression or defensiveness.

In addition, the quality of each of these four capacities deepens because gradually we notice that they are inseparable. We can only love with joy, compassion, and equanimity. We can only show compassion with love, joy, and equanimity, and so forth. We also realize that we humans are inseparable. Our compassion, for instance, is not dualistic, from us to those less fortunate. There is no separate self, no division between ourselves and others, so the sufferings of all are indeed our own.

The practice of loving-kindness is uniform, but each of us accomplishes it in our own unique way. Our qualities are the same, but our manner of manifesting of them is defined by our individual gifts, limits, and personal style. Following is a set of affirmations that foster our personal expression of loving-kindness and can be used throughout the day:

- I choose to love with all my might, in a style uniquely mine, here and now, always and everywhere, no one excluded.

- I act kindly toward others, not to impress or obligate them, but because I really am kind—or am working on it.

- If others fail to thank me or to return my kindness, that does not have to stop me from being loving nonetheless.

SUMMONING UP OUR COURAGE

Some of the commitments in this book may feel daunting or intimidating. As our dedication increases, we will ardently work on our fear reactions so that nothing can hold us back from conveying the integrity and loving-kindness that comprise our true nature.

Fear is not a verdict on us, or a sign of weakness, only a natural tendency that can be misdirected. Appropriate fear is a useful warning about threat and danger so that we can survive. Imaginary or self-stunting fear becomes an obstacle to our ability to thrive. Our primitive ancestors needed only to survive, so imaginary fear was useful since they never knew from which quarter danger might strike. But we can learn to deal with the self-stunting, neurotic fear that causes us pain and that limits our capacities.

We begin by acknowledging to ourselves that such misdirected fear will never go away completely, given its primitive origin. We cannot prevent ourselves from feeling fear ever again. But there is one thing we can do: we no longer have to act on our fear. The triple-A program—admit, allow, act—can help us:

We *admit* to ourselves and to someone we trust that we are afraid—rather than deny our fear, minimize it, or hide it.

We *allow* ourselves to feel our fear fully rather than try to drown it out with drugs or other escapes. Our focus is on how to hold our fear, not on how to get rid of it. We cradle our fear rather than treat it like a hot potato. We help this along not by criticizing or blaming ourselves for our fear but by taking it in stride as a default setting that all humans revert to sometimes. This reduces the power of fear, which thrives on the belief that we are isolated and alone.

We *act* in such a way that our fear does not drive us to do something or stop us from doing anything. (This "acting" is not in the sense of pretending but rather in the sense of behaving.) We are letting our fear be a companion who sits quietly in the passenger seat rather be than the reckless driver of our life.

Fear is a bully that takes advantage of powerlessness, the despair that happens when we believe that we have no options. The Triple A approach is an empowering option. Fear, like any bully, loses its capacity to threaten or torture us successfully when we stand up to it. No fighting is required, only standing at attention.

Finally, an undistracted focus prevents a fear reaction altogether. For example, in a crisis such as an earthquake, we are drawn directly into the experience and take some action without feeling fear. Our body is geared to survival, so at a time like that it goes into full-attention mode and does not allow fear to keep us from finding safety. It follows, therefore, that mindfulness practice has a direct impact on our ability to let go of our fear, because it keeps us focused on our immediate experience. Imagine the implications of this: the more we are here in the now, the less afraid we are of it—or anything.

PART ONE

Nurturing Ourselves

I

Safeguarding Our Health

OUR FIRST COMMITMENT to ourselves and our world is to care for our bodies. As responsible adults, we conduct our personal and professional lives in ways that safeguard our physical health. This includes staying fit through proper diet and exercise as well as steering clear of anything that we know can compromise our well-being. We hold to those activities and habits that support our health, and we are careful to monitor our stress level.

Our bodies cannot sustain work or activities that cause us so much stress that we are often exhausted or have no time to restore or recharge ourselves. It is therefore a good health practice to make decisions that lead to fewer encumbrances, more leisure, more recreation and fun.

We ask ourselves if our priorities have been lost in a whirlwind of pressures. We ask if we are running ourselves ragged in order to gain more of what is ultimately less valuable than our well-being. James Fox, abbot of the Trappist monastery at Gethsemani, said in a speech to his fellow Harvard Business School alumni, "I found myself asking, 'Is this what life is for, to burn it up in sweating, steaming, and toiling in a race for power, prestige, passion, pleasure, and piles of stocks and bonds, from every one of which I am going to be separated someday?'"

Here are some useful questions for contemplating your priorities and stress levels. A yes to any one of them is a call to attention and action:

- Am I usually exhausted when I come home from work?

- Am I doing more than my body can stand?

- Am I trying to maintain a lifestyle that is beyond my means?

- Have I bitten off more than I can chew in my attempt to maintain a certain status or income?

- Are my worries mounting?

- Have I fallen prey to addictions or compulsions?

- Is my work schedule adversely impacting my relationships?

- Am I neglecting the importance of time with my partner, family, friends?

- Am I neglecting the importance of time alone?

- Am I putting off a vacation or not feeling rested when I return from one?

- Is my mind so taken up with duties or work that I rarely find time to eat properly, relax adequately, or sleep long enough?

- Is what exhausts me more than can be cured by a night's sleep?

I am more and more conscious of my body and its signals to me. I am adjusting my diet, exercise, and habits to care for myself responsibly. I am not sacrificing my health to maintain a lifestyle that is beyond my means, geared to please others, or to gain status or fortune, which are the dead-end values in the ever-uneasy ego's world.

2

Our Psychological Self-Care

IN ADDITION TO CARING for our physical health, we can be attentive to our mental well-being—though they're usually closely linked, whether positively or negatively. Psychological self-care means focusing on how our lives can be happier and more effective, both personally and in relationships. This psychological work usually begins with examining what was not resolved in our past and how it affects us now. We then explore our present behavior to see how and if it is contributing to the achievement of our life goals. We also ask ourselves if our goals are accurately reflecting our own deepest needs and wishes. This is a lifelong process, and usually therapy can help us.

Our work may pivot around themes such as the following:

- How our childhood experiences have impacted our adult relationships and our self-esteem

- How fears, addictions, self-criticism, projections, illusions, or obsessions interfere with our serenity

- How our sense of safety, security, and support can come from within ourselves, as well as from others

- How comfortable we are with feelings, our own and those of others

- Whether guilt or shame inhibit us and how we look for ways to free ourselves

- Whether we have an excessive need to control others or to be controlled by them

- Whether we are sufficiently assertive rather than passive (or aggressive) in our ways of relating to others

- How willing we are to address, process, and resolve our inner and interpersonal conflicts

In exploring these areas we welcome the feelings that surround each of them. We pay attention to how they are related to past events and relationships. We notice if we have built ego defenses against knowing or showing our feelings, which are ultimately defenses against our own body.

We can engage in a courageous attentiveness to our full story and the patterns it has generated. Then we find it easier to let go of what has inhibited us and move on to what awaits us—the two requirements of a life journey.

Moving on in life is always a step toward adulthood. We are admitting humbly that we have work to do on ourselves and committing ourselves earnestly to doing it. We thereby access a sense of power that both raises our self-esteem and makes us more compassionate toward others. Our joy in that feels so much better than staying stuck that our steps forward turn into dance.

I am committed to working on myself, with help if need be, so that I can address, process, resolve, and integrate my emotional history, my conflicts, and my ongoing experiences. I am always looking for ways to let go of what is ready to go and move on to what comes next.

3

Grounded, Not Swayed

PSYCHOLOGICAL HEALTH includes going with the flow of life events without being destabilized by them. This happens when we can go through an experience as an honest witness, not as a judge, prosecutor, defendant, or victim. We notice what happens and how people behave with alertness and clarity—but without being thrown for a loop. We remind ourselves that we have dealt with crises, disappointments, and hurdles before and that this one is no exception. If necessary, we rally our support system, that is, our friends and guides who stand by us and help keep us on track. This is *equanimity, the ability to remain serene in the midst of what we cannot change.*

Our commitments to integrity and loving-kindness themselves equip us for any situation. Hence they are skillful means toward equanimity. Having more equanimity does not mean that the behavior of others or the events of life do not get to us. We feel the thud of what happens to us, but we are not totally devastated because of it. We let ourselves experience the feelings that are appropriate to what has happened but without becoming trapped in them or embittered by them.

We see ourselves as lightning rods: when strong feelings come up for us, we pause, acknowledge them, and imagine them flowing safely through our bodies from head to toe and then going to ground. This is what is meant by "remaining grounded": no longer thrown off course by events or by our reactions to them.

We further cultivate equanimity by applying two criteria to all our decisions: What offers serenity? What brings the fewest encumbrances? Equanimity follows as a natural result.

We grow in self-trust as we notice that we can deal with and feel anything while always coming back to our own center of sanity and repose thereafter. Soon we more easily believe that life unfolds in favor of our growth as long as we say yes to its knocks. This makes our predicaments and feelings valuable opportunities rather than negative, shameful, or ill-fated verdicts.

B. Alan Wallace, in *Buddhism with an Attitude*, writes, "The key to spiritual maturation is transforming all of life, adversity included, into spiritual practice." This is a way of understanding karma: all events, all people, and all they or we do produce consequences. The richest consequence is our opportunity to practice integrity and love.

The painful events in life have an impact on me, but they do not have to immobilize me. I look for ways to remain imperturbably secure within myself, trusting that I have access to many resources, within and around me, that help me handle what happens with equanimity. Now I see everything that happens to me, whether from people or events, as luminous opportunities to practice integrity and loving-kindness—and there is nothing left to fear.

4

Building Our Resources

THERE ARE HARD TIMES in everyone's life: Things go wrong, we are stressed, lonely, or down in the dumps. To cope with life's difficulties requires resources; self-soothing, self-protective, self-nurturing practices; and assets we can call on in time of need. These can be external, such as a support system or professional help. They can also be internal, competencies that help us in times of conflict, challenge, or danger. One of our adult tasks is to line up resources to have handy when we need them.

The Serenity Prayer, used in recovery programs (adapted from a prayer by the Protestant theologian Reinhold Niebuhr), goes, "God grant me the serenity to accept the things I cannot change, the courage to change the things I can, and the wisdom to know the difference." This prayer contains three of our key resources:

- When we accept what cannot be changed with an unconditional yes to the uncontrollable givens in life, we find the inner resource of *serenity*.

- When we take action to change what can be changed, we gain the inner resource of *courage*.

- When we assess the difference, we find the inner resource of *wisdom*.

Every practice in this book provides us with an inner resource. Each flows from one or more of those three options. Each helps us live in an adult, responsible, secure, and independent way.

We do not take care of ourselves when all we have lined up as our resources are *escapes* through unskillful choices such as addictions to substances or to sex, shopping, eating, or gambling. We can also be addicted to a person upon whom we have become dependent, no matter how dysfunctional the relationship may be.

Addiction sedates rather than soothes. It thrives on the illusory belief that there is something lasting out there that can get us through life's challenges unscathed, that can help us evade our grief for our losses or failures, that can sequester us from reality when it becomes uncomfortable, grant us a shortcut so we do not have to work on ourselves. Our practice, then, is to admit our powerlessness over our addictions and our need for assistance by joining a program of recovery that can restore us to sanity.

Addiction is not just an individual's problem but involves the whole family. Usually, without realizing it, partners and relatives have enabled an addict to continue in his behavior, so all need to take the steps that lead to healing. Programs of recovery include groups for everyone involved—another grace awaiting us.

I am gathering and building resources that help me face what life brings. I am keeping tabs on my use of what can or has become addictive. I am open to programs that can help me recover when I have an addiction or support me when a loved one suffers from one.

5

Letting Go of Regret

WE HAVE ALL MADE mistakes or committed indiscretions, be it in the realm of finance, career, relationship, or health. Sometimes, memories of one or more of these may arise out of nowhere as stabs of regret.

In those moments we can find practice opportunities: Regrets give us a comeuppance so that our ego can be kept from getting inflated. They are reminders of our fallibility. Our sense of ourselves can reduce from giant-size to life-size and we gain humility. We can practice loving-kindness toward ourselves, because regrets also give us an opportunity to be gentle toward our own mistakes: "May I not be hard on myself. May my regrets be reminders to forgive myself, learn from my mistakes, grow in humility, and be more careful in the future."

If our regret is about how we have harmed others, our practice is to make amends for our misdeeds, as long as doing so is not invasive or inappropriate. Otherwise we can say, "May [name the person we harmed] be happy now so that what I did in the past no longer harms him [or her] in any way."

If our regret is about how someone has hurt us, we might ask for amends or say, "May I be happy and forgiving now no matter how I was hurt in the past. May both of us act lovingly from now on." In this and in all our practices with regret we can add, "May all beings be happy in these same ways."

If we stick with this practice over time, regret and loving-kindness will become linked for us. If a regretful memory arises and we immediately add the practice just described, or remind ourselves of our having done so in the past, it comes back next time with that optimistic add-on. We have linked regretting to resolving and the two come back in one cluster.

Now regret cannot dead-end us into a useless sense of shame, making us lose sight of our positive qualities. When regrets no longer victimize us but become triggers to the healing power of spiritual practice, we are encouraged rather than repudiated. We begin to see all that has happened in our lives with detached amusement and committed compassion.

As I struggle with regret or self-reproach because of the mistakes I have made in life, I am no longer ashamed of my fallibility. I regard my errors as learning experiences so I can do better in the future. My regrets about how I have hurt others lead me to make amends wherever I can. My mistakes are thus becoming a valuable passport to humility and to tender compassion toward myself and others. I may always feel regrets, but now I have a program to work with them so that they can be allies, not enemies. My mind may shoot arrows of regret at me from time to time, but I am using them to open my heart, not to wound it.

6

Auditing Our Beliefs

IT's WORTHWHILE to look carefully at the beliefs, principles, and values we have gained from the many sources in our lives, including family, religion, and society. Our practice can be to examine all that we have believed or now believe so that we can appreciate what has helped us to evolve.

This process becomes complete when we also clean house—the inner house of our mind that waits to be updated and freed of superstition, self-stunting beliefs, and prejudice. We can ask which attitudes and values serve our growth and which are ready to be dispensed with. This doesn't mean having fewer firm values, but honing the values we have so that they mesh better with who we are today and become resources for growing in integrity and love.

This list may help us in performing an honest audit of our beliefs. Healthy, loving, growth-promoting values and beliefs are those that:

- Harmonize with recent discoveries in science, psychology, and spirituality

- Keep directing us to reality rather than wishful thinking or candy-coated views

- Teach us that life is about happiness with responsibility, not simply the enduring of pain

- Prompt us to act with self-nurturance, unconditional integrity, and universal loving-kindness

- Ensure freedom of intellect, voice, and choice so that we have individual authority over the shape of our beliefs and our conscience

- Suggest moral principles that accommodate the full range of legitimate human behavior rather than keep us inhibited or inappropriately ashamed of our wishes or actions

- Give us a love of learning and inquiry so that we are always open to new ideas rather than becoming dogmatic or doctrinaire

- Help us respect reasonable limits and conventions but also question the authorities whose legitimacy we base not on their claims to extraordinary powers but on their concern for our continual maturation

- Free us from biases against race, sexual orientation, gender, or a particular religious or political persuasion

- Increase our awareness of world concerns and animate us to become engaged in action that promotes justice, peace, liberty, equality, and love

- Challenge us as well us support us

- Keep us aware of and thankful for the gifts and graces that come to us

---

I am thankful for the set of values I received in the course of my life from so many sources. At the same time, I am examining the scaffolding of beliefs, values, and assumptions that I inherited from family, school, religion, and society. One by one, I seek to dismantle and discard those that are not in keeping with mature adult living and cherish those that are.

PART TWO

Cultivating Our Integrity

7

Honoring Agreements and Boundaries

OTHERS TRUST US when they know that if we agree to do something, we can be trusted to do it. We do not forget, renege, or procrastinate. We also respect ourselves more as we become people who keep our word.

If it becomes clear to us that a task we agreed to do has turned out to be too much for us, we do not keep at it "even if it kills us." We admit that we overcommitted ourselves and we negotiate a more reasonable plan. In this way, we do not compromise our own needs nor do we leave others in the lurch.

We are honoring our own boundaries when we are assertive enough to declare, beforehand or later, that a task is too much for us or that we choose not to do it.

We honor others' boundaries by being careful not to create in them a dependency on us. This can happen when we overly care-take others—including keeping our grown children unlaunched.

Here are practices that protect our boundaries and honor those of others:

- Acting cooperatively while paying attention to our own needs and plans

- Doing more for others only when doing so leads to helpful changes in their behavior and activates them to take care of themselves

- Contributing to a project but not doing all the work

- Asking that endeavors be reciprocal

- Basing our contribution on explicit agreements and negotiations

- Offering assistance because we want to and not allowing ourselves to be guilt-tripped or manipulated into doing what we do not really want to do, especially by threats of abandonment

- Being able, guiltlessly, to say "no," "enough," or "stop"

- Remaining free agents rather than being at the mercy or beck and call of others

- Assertively and respectfully expressing to others what we feel, think, and want

- Handling money matters—loans, for example—with caution and objectivity

- Giving generously but reasonably and then letting go

I do my best to keep my word, honor my commitments, and follow through on the tasks I agree to do. At the same time, I set reasonable limits and boundaries on how I do this. I no longer make promises for the sake of pleasing or appeasing others. I want to be generous, not out of obligation, but by choice.

8

Honest and True

WE CAN CHOOSE to be honorable, truthful, and trustworthy in all our dealings. We do not engage in deceit, mendacity, fraud, scheming, or trickery. We are not comfortable with any transaction unless both we and the other are satisfied with the way a deal is designed. We do not seek to cheat anyone, pull the wool over anyone's eyes, or get away with something.

As we are no longer swayed by opportunities for quick gain or self-promotion at the expense of others, we are less likely to transgress our boundaries or act foolishly, callously, or immorally. *We cherish the joy of a good conscience more than any material benefit.* Indeed, the happiness resulting from our commitment to integrity and love can become more valuable than any financial or personal aggrandizement. We are seeing our definitions of success, happiness, and gain reframed in a spiritual way.

As we grow in spiritual consciousness, we act in accord with standards we can be proud of, no matter what advantage we might thereby miss out on. What matters to us is an upright life, not glee at how we put one over on someone or "made a bundle." Our freedom from such seductions has become much more valuable than whether we make a killing or stay on top. Now the "top" has come to look like the heaven of a communion of humanity, the best position from which to show love, rather than the summit from which we look down on others or chuckle over having more than they do.

If we have acted in dishonest ways, we are committed to acknowledging our errors, making restitution, acting differently in the future—spiritual practices that help us grow in humility and fairness.

This way of living opens us to a new sense of what happiness can mean. It is no longer conditional, based on the pleasures that can come our way. Real happiness is unconditional, not based on what is happening around us. Now we are happy independently because we have and act on principles no matter how others may behave or how undeserving they may seem.

Finally, this commitment results in no longer being at the mercy of others' opinions. We are satisfied when we have acted in a conscientious way no matter whether other people notice or whether they misunderstand our motivations. We then notice a sigh of relief welling up in us since we longer have to jump in to explain ourselves, head off others' criticism, or mend their impressions of us. In any case, we are always ready to clarify our intentions or declare our truth when appropriate, and we accept that what others do with our truth is beyond our control.

I am making sincere attempts to abide by standards of rigorous honesty, and fair play in all my dealings, no matter how others act toward me or what they believe about me. My question is not "What can I get away with?" but "What is the right thing to do?" If I fall down in this, I can admit it, make amends, and resolve to act differently the next time.

9

Awareness of Influences

LIKE DISNEY'S PINOCCHIO, we sometimes meet up with tricksters who have predatory skill and can persuade us to act against our better judgment or to believe we want or need what is not really necessary. We can become more aware of the subtle impact such forces have on our behavior and choices.

We can choose to become particularly alert to the omnipresent influences of the three main streets that direct so many attitudes and lifestyles: Madison Avenue, Wall Street, and Hollywood Boulevard.

We can work on becoming less materialistic by remaining aware of how the Madison Avenue advertising industry seeks to make us want what they say we have to have. We can free ourselves from being driven by Wall Street's compulsive style of amassing ever more money, whether or not we really need it or whether the means used to produce it were worthy. We can enjoy entertainment but notice how Hollywood may commandeer us into espousing superficial or unenlightened values such as glamour, extravagance, and thrills. We do not have to feel inadequate when we do not have the looks, wealth, heady romance, power, or attractive partners we see in movies and on television.

Moving away from these three streets, we choose instead to take our stand where the boulevards of Mindfulness and Loving-kindness meet. There we have let go of the need to grab and hold, because pomp and promise cannot seduce us to want more and more. Becoming more sincere and more loving has become the "more" we seek.

On that corner, free of vanity, we dress as we choose, not compelled to sport the latest fashion—unless we genuinely like it. We arrive in the vehicle that fits our needs, rather than the one that makes the biggest impression. We choose the restaurant where we can find wholesome food, not the trendy one where we can be seen. We have all we need just as we are.

Our practice of loving-kindness toward all the squatters on "the three main streets" is our aspiration that all of us cherish goodness over goods or glitz. This kindly concern has canceled any envy we might feel and turns our hearts toward compassion without smugness, disdain, or any sense of superiority.

I can now measure my success by how much steadfast love I have, not by how much I have in the bank, how much I achieve in business, or how glamorous my life is. Wholesomeness and love are becoming more vital, rewarding, and exciting than anything I can gain from things, money, or thrills.

10

Not Taking Advantage

WE MAY NOTICE that we have an upper hand in some interactions because we have more knowledge or ability than someone else. We may also have more skill in persuasion or more power by reason of status or economic advantage. We may notice that someone is vulnerable because she is at low ebb, in crisis, depressed, gullible, or needy.

A person of character and standards will not take advantage of any of this. She will act with integrity and compassion, not exploiting the situation. The practice is to act from compassion for another's plight, wanting to help him get back on his feet before we enter into transactions with him, since we want to operate only on an equal playing field. This requires our caring more about being fair than about what we can acquire.

We also grow in integrity as we receive from others

without taking too much from them. They may not know how to set appropriate limits on their sharing. We show compassion when we do not let others deplete themselves to be of service to us. We are not "takers."

Being a "taker" may have psychological roots. If we were deprived emotionally in childhood, we may now be left with a feeling that there is still something coming to us, something we're owed. We may believe that things or money can substitute for emotional goods, especially if we have given up on ever finding the love we want.

Our taking advantage of others may arise from feeling entitled to have others come through for us. We may even imagine that we can take from them unfairly. Overcoming all this requires psychological work—addressing, processing, and resolving the conflict we are having with regard to giving and receiving.

We know we are on the spiritual path when we realize that the goodness in us calls us to be stewards, not predators, of those who are impoverished in some way. We also come to see that others are not required to give to us, though we appreciate it when they do.

We learn to take care of ourselves and at the same time are glad when others pitch in to help us. We do the same for them.

We express our thanks to others for giving to us out of the goodness of their hearts, not because something is owed to us.

When we develop a truly unconditional and caring generosity, the sense of being owed, like the sense of owing and the right to take advantage, all vanish.

I forgo taking advantage of anyone because of his or her ignorance, status, or financial straits. I let go of any belief that others owe me something or are expected to take care of me. More and more, I am taking care of myself and showing respect and kindness to those who need me.

11

Respecting the Lineup

ONE OF THE STERNEST givens of life is that we don't always come first—even if we seem to deserve it. This may be difficult for the arrogant or entitled ego to accept. Humility means accepting our place in line even though we may believe we deserve to be ahead of others. Patiently standing in a queue at the store is a simple and helpful practice for learning this. We do not push others aside; rather we honor their place—and ask that they honor ours. We thereby combine respect for others' rights with protection of our own.

The spiritual practice of saying yes to the various lineups we encounter in life does not mean that we do not compete at all, only that we do not do so in a cutthroat way. Our respect for ourselves and for our life's work allows us to get ahead; our caring for others does not let us step on them to get there.

Saying yes to the reality of where we are in the moment makes us feel more at home in the world, because we are not comparing ourselves with others. Our experiences then become vivid opportunities for the following:

- We acknowledge that others may have more to offer in certain areas than we do.

- We feel pride in our unique talents and accomplishments.

- We are learning to question the motivation behind our ego-compulsion to "get there first," to reach the top of the ladder, to have more than anyone just for the sake of having it.

- Our glee in competition turns into the joy of cooperation.

- We can be happy about the successes of others. The more we realize that each of us is here to make his or her own unique contribution to the evolution of all of us, the happier we are that someone found a way to do his or her part.

- On the family level, our sibling rivalry has vanished. We now accept that parents sometimes have favorites or like one child more than another. If we were the privileged one, we feel for our siblings. If we were not, we grieve, let go of blame or resentment, and say yes to the family lineup as it was. We treat our brothers and sisters as equals and ask for the same.

- Regarding our present position in a career or relationship, we are always working toward advancement while behaving respectfully toward others.

- We are grounded in an empowering sense of safety and security based on the world that is, ourselves as we are, others as they are, not on the cutthroat world the ego so desperately craves, invents, or demands.

I am choosing not to push others aside so that I can get ahead. I choose neither to exalt myself nor to abase myself. Instead, I take my turn, without complaint, at being first, last, or midway in the long series of lineups that life has in store for all of us.

12

Our Inventory

COMPANIES COMMITTED to honesty welcome regular audits of their policies, assets, and liabilities. Similarly, we can take a written inventory to audit our personal integrity. We include not only a focus on our failings but also an assessment of the ways in which we are successfully acting with integrity, using our gifts, showing our love. In a journal, we can list the following:

- The times we did not act with honesty and integrity

- How we have not utilized the gifts and talents we know we possess

- The biases we hold within ourselves toward those we perceive to be different—whether or not we have acted on them

- The times we recall having hurt others intentionally or failed to face or forgive those who have hurt us

After taking this inventory, we can promise to ourselves, and in the presence of a person we trust, that we will change our behavior for the future.

Next we can take a positive inventory of ourselves, listing the following:

- How we have maintained honesty, trustworthiness, and sincerity in our dealings with others

- How we have activated our gifts and potentials

- How we have been inclusive of and welcoming toward others, especially those who are different from ourselves

- How we have acted generously toward others

- How we are seeking reconciliation with those who are in disputes with us

- How we are showing forgiveness (letting go of blame and vindictiveness) toward those who have hurt us

We share this inventory as well with a friend or confidant. We welcome an acknowledgment of our shortcomings as well as an appreciation of our virtues and strengths.

This practice can have three useful consequences: We

grow in humility as we recognize our failings. We grow in self-respect as we amend them. We grow in self-esteem as we appreciate our powers. Such freeing of ourselves from self-doubt and self-criticism is showing loving-kindness to ourselves.

I examine my conscience regularly. I am taking searching inventories not only about how I may not have acted with integrity but also about how I may have hurt others, how I may not have launched or shared my gifts, how I may still be holding on to prejudices or the will to retaliate, how I may still not be as loving, inclusive, and open as I can be. I also appreciate myself for the times when I have activated my potentials, acted with integrity, and shown my big-hearted love.

PART THREE

Becoming As Real As We Can Be

13

Saying Yes to Reality

LIFE HAS CERTAIN GIVENS, certain unavoidable facts. Five stand out for all of us: Everything changes and ends; things do not always go according to our plans; life is not always fair; suffering is part of everyone's life; people are not always loving, honest, generous, loyal—nor can they be expected to be.

An unconditional yes to these facts of life is a surrender to what is. This is not resignation or giving up. It is aligning ourselves to reality with calm ruthlessness. We then find the wisdom to see the difference between what can and what cannot be changed. We do all we can to change the things that can be changed and, with equal alacrity, to accept whatever cannot be changed. We are serene in unalterable circumstances because we are no longer beleaguered by the stress of being at odds with them.

The opposite of saying yes is seeking control. We try to control other people, our own feelings, and life events. In facing life as it is, the style of yes is to let the chips fall where they may and then play them to the best benefit of ourselves and others.

As we practice our unconditional yes, without protest or complaint, we notice that we no longer ask, "Why?" or "Why me?" Now we simply say, "Yes, now what?" This is a giant step into adulthood because our focus is on how to move on with our life, not on how immobilized we are as victims. We also gain humility because we finally depose the exalted ego from its illusory rank of potentate over all that happens.

The foundation of the practice of yes is a dauntless trust that the laws of the universe do indeed serve an evolutionary purpose. We trust that the events in and conditions of our life are the very factors that can give us depth, character, and compassion. Yes to what is means yes to what we can be.

Nonetheless, the givens of life represent losses to us. Our innate technology for handling losses is grief. We feel sad when life is hard on us; we feel angry that bad things can happen to us; we feel afraid that we may not survive in the school of hard knocks. Grieving involves a letting go that leads directly to moving on. We can trust not only life as it unfolds but also ourselves as being capable of facing what is unfolding. We have given up the self-made suffering that comes from complaining about life's givens in favor of accepting the life-made suffering that nourishes our growth. This growth occurs when we embrace whatever happens to us as an opportunity for the practice of mindfulness, for addressing, processing, and resolving our conflicts, for living in integrity and loving-kindness.

I am learning to say yes to the givens of life without protest, complaint, or blame. As I land on concrete reality rather than hang on to wishful thinking, I notice I am less apt to cling to what is passing or run from what is arising. I greet the passing with a good-bye, the oncoming with a yes, and both with thanks.

14

Just As We Are

MOST OF US LEARN, early in our lives, how to posture and pose. We design a persona, a way of portraying ourselves to others that we think will be satisfactory to them. We may have begun constructing this false self in childhood, especially if it was not safe to be ourselves, just as we were, in our family. We may still be trying to fashion our behavior to others' liking.

There is another alternative: we ourselves can become the audience that matters to us. That happens when we give up any attempts to get others to accept or love us. We still build and use social skills, but we are unwilling to change ourselves in order to fit in. Instead, we want to portray ourselves realistically, no matter what the reaction of others.

We are aware of our limitations—and are working on

them. We hope others will do the same, but we do not try to make that happen. In fact, we do not want to use any charms of body, word, or mind to trick or seduce others into wanting us. We are pleased with others' attraction to us only when it is for us just as we are. We are applying our practice of the unconditional yes to the givens of our appearance, lifestyle, and personality.

We notice two results: We are no longer intimidated by the judgments of others. Others then find us more appealing because we show that we like ourselves and, at the same time, appreciate them. This is the exquisite paradox in how being ourselves leads to more connection to others.

Our practice of becoming more authentic makes us more accommodating toward and patient with ourselves, which are forms of loving-kindness. As we settle into the reality of who we are, with pride in our gifts and unabashed awareness of our limits, we more easily access happiness, sanity, and wisdom.

Others love us more because our courage and vulnerability are more appealing to them than successful pretense. We love ourselves more because our own unconditional truthfulness has become more valuable to us than praise.

I desire so to conduct the affairs of this administration that if, at the end, when I come to lay down the reins of power, I have lost every other friend on earth, I shall at least have one friend left, and that friend shall be down inside of me.

—ABRAHAM LINCOLN, "Speech to the Missouri Committee of Seventy"

———————

I am letting go of the need to keep up appearances or to project an overly impressive self-image. I am becoming ever more willing to appear as I am, without pretense and no matter how unflattering. Being loved for who I am has become more important—and more interesting—than upholding the ever-shaky status of my persona in the world.

———————

15

Respectful Assertiveness

As we grow emotionally and spiritually, we learn to be assertive rather than aggressive in our dealings with others. This means the following:

- We are clear about our needs and motives. We ask for what we want, but we do not attempt, directly or indirectly, to manipulate others. We can hear a no and accept it, rather than pushing or harassing others to bend to our will.

- We take responsibility for our own feelings. We show our feelings directly and nonintrusively. We are open to the feelings of others but do not accept abuse. We ask that others respect our boundaries and choices. We honor the individual and relationship boundaries of others.

- We show respect for the timing of others by not insisting that they respond as we would or act as quickly as we might like. We accept the given that everyone operates on a unique timetable and we show patience and respect for this variety in human responsiveness.

We see that "aggression" does not refer only to violence, injury, or attack. Our aggression shows up in relationships when we control, bully, criticize, demand, or blame. Aggression is the opposite of assertiveness since it fails to honor others' freedom. It is the opposite of love, which includes acceptance of others as they are and allows them the space to make and live out their own choices.

Some of our aggression toward others is based on our fears and frustrations. We may then act unkindly, and it is up to us to apologize. At other times, our aggression is malicious. We are deliberately hurtful and mean. We want to cause harm. That is a spiritual malady rather than a neurotic reaction or a poor social skill. It requires conversion, a deep and radical reformation of ourselves. Our part will be to commit ourselves to the spiritual practices of making amends, reconciling, and opening to the grace of transformation.

Finally, we are aggressive toward ourselves when we do not disbar the inner critic who judges us too harshly. We can learn from the style of the gentle practices in this book. They show trust in our goodness while acknowledging the need for practices that help us show it and make amends when we fail to show it. We can be that kind of well-meaning assessor of ourselves.

I am learning to ask for what I need without demand, manipulation, or expectation. I honor the timing, wishes, and limits of others while protecting my own boundaries. I am open to a radical transformation of myself so that I can be free of malice. I look for ways to be kind to myself while not letting myself get away with anything.

16

Admitting Our Failings

IN OUR COMMITMENT to living life with integrity and loving-kindness, we keep an eye on ourselves. We are willing to admit it when we notice that we are not living up to these commitments. If we see that we have just lied, attempted to manipulate, or acted in a selfish or unkind way, we own up to it immediately.

We are open about our motives, no matter how embarrassing. For example, we might stop ourselves in mid-sentence and admit to someone, "Don't be fooled by my manner. I'm acting as if I were definite and on top of things when, in reality, I doubt myself." Using another example we might say, "I'm asking if you want to go to the movies with me not only because I enjoy your company but because I'm lonely." Such a ruthlessly candid confession increases our humility—and winsomeness. Such honest self-presentation—and others' appreciation of it—

comes to matter more to us than how well we have hidden our true motives.

Feeling embarrassed is sometimes a requirement for the practices that help us to change. The ability to endure the sting of embarrassment enables us to act authentically. When we know we have committed ourselves to ante up about our phoniness and that it will embarrass us to do so, we are more likely to choose the path of genuineness to begin with. The pain of showing ourselves, warts and all, is not as distressing as that of admitting our phoniness, especially to people we do not want to be vulnerable to in that way.

There is often a double standard lurking behind the propensity to be false. For instance, we might be aggressive and unapologetic at home but quite accommodating and courteous at work. As we grow in integrity and loving-kindness, we choose to be consistent, the same at home as at work, with strangers as with friends.

As we own up to our falsenesses, others will respect us for our frankness. But that is not our motivation. We do this to become more transparent, not more admired. Some forms of nakedness may lead to disgrace, but this form of exposure leads to the grace of self-acceptance. We come to realize that our inadequacies do not have to be a source of self-recrimination or shame.

Eventually, we will trust ourselves so much—and find such delight in being authentic—that we will want everything we do to reveal us, no matter what the reactions or consequences. We will then become more aware of the extent of our goodness and our invincibility in the face of any fear. When there is nothing left to hide or run from we find our real freedom. It was under our heap of inhibitions and cautions waiting for release.

———————————

More and more, I blow the whistle on myself when I notice that I am being phony, aggressive, or manipulative. I want to come clean right then and there by admitting that I am acting falsely. I am transparent choosing to be more authentic and consistent in all my relationships. Now I more easily and willingly apologize when necessary. In all these ways I begin to believe in my inherent goodness and to act on it.

———————————

17

Tracking Our Reactions

IT IS A GIVEN that people sometimes upset us. However, in some cases our reaction is more intense than an event warrants. Our discomfort or resentment can hang on and gnaw at us. Such holding on may be pointing to something unnoticed and unaddressed in ourselves rather than to the actions of the other person. We can SEE what is going on with us by asking ourselves whether our *shadow*, *ego*, or *early-life experience* has been triggered:

1. Is this my *shadow*? We may neglect or disavow traits in ourselves that seem unacceptable to society or even to ourselves. Carl Jung called this the "shadow." It can also be positive traits that we disown, such as our own potential for talent, virtue, and self-expansion.

We are stopped or driven by what we keep unconscious. Our shadow begins to become conscious when we catch ourselves in the act of projecting it onto others. For example, we may strongly dislike others whose behavior actually displays our own negative traits. Or, on the other hand, we may strongly admire those who showcase gifts that resemble our own untapped potential.

We can ask if what has upset us is similar to our own hidden, disavowed, or unnoticed qualities, and begin to acknowledge them in ourselves. Our question here: "Is what I'm disliking in others a quality that I also have, but have difficulty acknowledging?"

2. Is this my *ego*? Our ego can be so inflated that we bristle at others' failure to respect us in the exact way we require. We are aroused to fury or indignation when our "greatness" is not honored, when our shortcomings are pointed out to us, no matter how kindly meant, or when we are not given our way, no matter how undeserved. Our neurotic ego reacts to exposure of its limits with defensiveness, making openness to self-examination impossible. This ego's favorite sport is retaliation, making human connection and forgiveness improbable. We can notice our reactions, calm down, accept our fallibility, and open to the world of equal footing with others. Our question here: "Am I upset because this is bruising my defensive ego?"

3. Is this from my *early life*? Is this person or situation reminding me of childhood pain or disappointment that has never been resolved? Our unfinished business from childhood may come to the fore when someone reminds us of how one of our parents treated us. We may react to someone as if he were a parent or other significant figure

from our past. We are transferring archaic feelings or expectations onto the present. We can notice such transference and work on our emotional baggage, perhaps in therapy, to help undo the past rather than redo it. Our question here: "Is this reminding me of my past?"

Any strong reaction I have to others is becoming a summons to look at my own behavior and traits, an opportunity for a sincere and defenseless exploration of myself.

18

Our Gifts and Our Bliss

IT'S IMPORTANT to appreciate our innate talents. It is never too late to begin using our gifts, and it is always too early to give up on them. We can put energy into using our gifts in the work we do and for the accomplishment of our life goals.

A sense of accomplishment is a source of bliss. We feel a boost to our self-esteem when we give ourselves credit for work well done and when we receive compliments from others. We feel good about ourselves as individuals when we have something to show for our work. We feel good as partners and family members when we grow in the arts of love and intimacy. Our successes in our work and relationships are like a woodpile neatly cut and stacked by us.

Not all of us have the privilege of having a job that gives us a sense of accomplishment and of making a contribution—both of which are sources of satisfaction. We might need to look at our work life and ask where we go from here. We can maintain our belief in the possibility of change for the better by not giving up on seeking the work we truly enjoy. At the same time, we can be realistic about our chances. If we cannot find work that feeds our soul, we can have a hobby, project, or avocation that does. This may be difficult when we do not know our own inner needs. The following questions may help us find out what they are:

- What are my gifts and talents and how does my lifestyle include and advance them?

- What has consistently brought me happiness and a sense of fulfillment?

- What in my life arises from choice and what from obligation?

- What do I admire or envy in the lifestyle of others?

- What would I like to see happen for those I love? (This is often a clue to what we want for ourselves.)

- What am I being encouraged to do or be by those I trust?

- What am I afraid of risking if I "break out of the box"?

- What are the loves and longings I am afraid to tell anyone about and why?

- What will it take for me to believe that it is my turn to make the choices that reflect who I am and what makes me happy?

- What is being communicated to me about my gifts and my bliss through meaningful coincidences and dreams?

I am enthusiastically seeking, or am thankful to have found, meaningful work and projects. I have reason to be proud of my accomplishments. Henry David Thoreau wrote in his journal, "A man looks with pride at his woodpile." I see my choices for self-nurturance, integrity, and love as my "woodpile."

PART FOUR

Being with Others

19

Respecting Lifestyles
and Customs

OUR CHOSEN LIFESTYLE is a reflection of our own deepest needs, values, and wishes. We can honor the lifestyles and customs of others, no matter how different they may be from our own. Abraham Maslow, in his study of self-actualized people, reported, "The self-actualized person will go through the rituals of convention with a good-humored shrug and the best possible grace." That shrug is a spiritual act since it shows respect for others and an openness to the diversity of human experience.

Our individuality is in no way diminished by participating in the harmless rituals that mean a lot to others, especially those of a former generation, such as calling or going home on holidays or at times of illness or death in the family. As we become gracious about what others cherish, we may feel more loved by those who notice our openness. That response is not our motivation (in this or in any of the practices in this book). We participate in social rituals not as a strategy to achieve love or approval but because sharing in activities that mean a lot to others is an important way we can show our love.

It may also happen that when we visit or call family members, they berate or attack us because of our lifestyle and the choices that have differed from theirs. Healthy self-respect will not permit us to be scolded or shamed for who we are, no matter how close the relationship. We do not defend ourselves, try to convince, or retaliate in reaction to such rebukes by others. We simply excuse ourselves without blaming them and then keep our further contacts to the barest necessary minimum. Our love is unconditional, but our willingness to maintain contact depends on our being treated respectfully.

As we commit ourselves to being loving in all our dealings, we do not choose permanent rifts in communication. As soon as others begin to show sincere respect and openness toward us, we increase our contact. If others cut us off, we grieve and honor their decision while also making it clear that if they want to reconcile, we are always willing. We accept sudden unexplained silences or disappearances by others and never use that style ourselves. Connection and reconnection are important to us, but only when we feel safe. Maintaining our safety is loving-kindness toward ourselves.

I am willing to participate in the conventions and social rituals that make others happy. If family or friends disparage my lifestyle, I continue to care about them but I keep my contact minimal. I remain open to reconciling with those from whom I have distanced myself or who have distanced themselves from me. And no one I know or have known will ever be omitted from my meditative practice of loving-kindness.

20

Open to Feedback

WE CAN BENEFIT from knowing how we affect others and how we come across to them. We can free ourselves from the disability of not being open to candid feedback. We can practice opening to any truth about ourselves that comes from the sincere estimations of others. At the same time, we do not have to swallow others' opinions whole and we refuse to be insulted or attacked by anyone.

A discerning and welcoming spirit arises in us when we become so intent on working on ourselves that we *want* to know where our failings and limitations lie. Then we can adjust our behavior for the better. With this as our motivation, we check in with others. We ask whether we are or have been unkind, untrue, or unwise, since love and wisdom have come to matter most to us. The Zen master Wuzu wrote, "The ancients were always so glad to hear of their mistakes."

Gradually, our self-esteem increases because we notice that we care more about living truthfully and lovingly than about being seen by others as perfect. Paradoxically, this style of healthy humility makes us more appealing to others. A power becomes visible in us when we are no longer putting up a fight against our own transformation but are opening ourselves to it—in any form it may take or from any source that helps us get there.

Some of us find it difficult to receive *positive* feedback. We may shy away from compliments, compassion, and caring, no matter how well deserved or needed. We may feel uncomfortable because of the closeness that happens when someone likes or admires us. We may be suspicious of the motives of those who genuinely appreciate us. These are all forms of fear that stunt the growth of our self-esteem and our relationships. The practice is simply to keep eye contact with the person who honors us and say, "Thank you."

It is a legitimate practice to ask for appreciation from others in the same way that we check in with them about our negative behavior. We are looking for ways to be supported in our practice. We want to let love in. This is as important as—and often more challenging than—sending love out.

Our best example is the cat. She receives all our petting, purring for more, even arching her body to make sure our caresses reach every deserving part of her. In our relationships with others, do we fear being touched by appreciation and affection?

I am learning to open myself to others' sincere and well-meant feedback rather than becoming defensive or ego-reactive to it. When someone points out that I have been unkind or inauthentic, I am not defensive but simply take it as information about what I have to work on. At the same time, I appreciate positive feedback and say, "Thanks."

21

Healthy Anger

BECOMING A MORE LOVING person doesn't mean that we don't get angry; it means that we express it in healthy ways. When someone hurts us, we find a clear way of saying, "Ouch!" and "No more of that!" alerting the other person to the impact of his or her behavior. Perhaps this person did not realize that her actions were causing pain. We can help her see that. On the other hand, if she intended to inflict pain on us, she needs to know that such behavior is not OK.

In this practice, we do not make others wrong or seek revenge. We are simply communicating our hurt to someone and setting clear limits for future interactions. We do not let others walk all over us. We also resist the impulse to pass on the hurt or to make others feel as bad as we do. Our practice can be threefold: stating our pain, not hurting back, and not staying in situations that prolong pain.

Healthy anger is displeasure at actions that we perceive as unfair. Our practice is to express our anger without being abusive. This means that we maintain control of ourselves—we do not lose our temper but manage it. We express our anger with a motivation to repair the bond, not to hurt the other back. We take responsibility for how we interpreted what happened and for the feelings that arose in us. The other person is seen to be a catalyst for our anger, not the cause of it.

The abusive and aggressive style of anger is adversarial, blaming, out-of-control, and retaliatory. We lose our temper and attempt to intimidate the person who we believe has wronged us. We see the other not as a peer but as a target. We demand change rather than ask for it. We do not work toward repair of the relationship, only getting our rage out, no matter who gets hurt.

Appropriate anger is focused on the act that seemed unfair. Abusive anger is more widespread and related to how affronted our ego feels and how it can save face. Healthy anger is brief and is let go of so that we can continue relating. The abusive style lingers as resentment, and injures or ends the relationship.

Our ultimate commitment is to a style in human relating that keeps no record of wrongs. This is the opposite of hatred, rage, or an insatiable need to keep punishing so that no resolution of the conflict is possible. Some people feel ongoing hatred, which is a sad and dangerous condition to be possessed by. Healthy people do not hate, because their commitment is to reconciling whenever possible, to resolving rage rather than letting it hang on as unappeasable vindictiveness.

I do not choose to hurt or hate anyone. If someone hurts me, I can say, "Ouch!" open a dialogue, and ask for amends. I am giving up the primitive, gangland style of retaliation in favor of practicing healthy anger, not letting others abuse me, and looking for ways to bring about harmony.

22

How We Can Include

A GROUP OR FAMILY that provides a sense of safety and security is called a "holding environment." In it we feel accepted and protected, supported and sheltered. Most of us are terrified of becoming outsiders, cut off from that sense of belonging, which is a primal need in all of us.

An unfortunate style for some people is to adhere to the distinction between "insider" and "outsider" as a way of assuring a personal sense of safety. "Insider versus outsider" is an invention of the primitive ego, still meta-phorically huddling around campfires for safety in a per-ilous world. We can give up the primitive form of shelter that insider groups offer in favor of the joy of reaching out to the human community without exception. We can decline membership in groups that exclude. The fol-lowing poem, "Outwitted" by Edwin Markham, can be our affirmation:

He drew a circle that shut me out—
Heretic, a rebel, a thing to flout.
But Love and I had the wit to win:
We drew a circle that took him in!

Gossiping about someone can make us feel like insiders, while the other becomes the outsider. The warmth and comfort we feel when we do this is coming from the archaic, tribal campfire, not from the heart. Part of becoming more spiritually aware is giving up primitive versions of safety and security, those that happen at the expense of others.

Our style of addressing, processing, and resolving can be an alternative to gossiping. We practice addressing when we bring up issues face-to-face with the person involved. We process our questions and concerns by sharing our feelings directly with that person. We resolve our issues as we move toward an understanding between us without leftover resentment. This is an example of how a psychological tool has a spiritual dimension. It awakens more compassion in us toward those who are considered outcasts. It makes us less attached to being insiders.

We see the insider-outsider distinction so often in jobs, families, nations, religions, and politics. Spiritually aware people have come to see that such division is a barrier to secure connection and a threshold into a life of fear. Our inclusive communicative practices take us jubilantly beyond such limiting options. We come to appreciate the indivisible. We welcome and want to be part only of what is all-inclusive, free of label, category, or rank.

I notice that in some groups, there are people who are put down, demeaned, or excluded. Rather than be comforted that I am still an insider, especially by gossiping about them, I want to sense the pain of those who are outsiders and include everyone in my circle of love and respect.

23

Our Sense of Humor

HEALTHY HUMOR pokes gentle fun at human foibles and ironic contradictions, especially our own. The negative side of humor is sarcasm, ridicule, teasing, mocking, demeaning or taunting others, and prejudicial jokes about individuals or groups. Even when this is meant to be all in fun, it is hurtful language and not part of the repertory of those committed to a loving style of speech.

We can decide not to engage in—or to listen approvingly to—negative humor. Our assertiveness can help us speak up about our discomfort with jokes that show hatred or bigotry.

We maintain custody over what we say so that we do not hurt or humiliate anyone. We are then making loving-kindness more important than how entertaining we can be. We notice how our words land on others. We also forgo engaging in practical jokes or tricks. Our aspiration might be the following: "May I be free of aggression and may I detect every subtle form it takes."

We let others know that we are choosing not to engage in hurtful humor and ask them to speak up if they see us flagging in our resolve. In this way, friends are more than a team of insiders. They are referees and coaches too.

When someone is sarcastic toward us, we are not quick with a zinger reply. Instead, we open a dialogue about what may really be going on. Perhaps someone's true anger at us will then be lured from its dark hiding place in so-called humor and we can address it together directly. Negative humor is a favorite weapon of those who are indirect or passive. We become healthier when we become direct and active in our communication, two more ways to show respect for others.

When we apply loving-kindness to our speech and behavior, we are doing more than simply wishing others happiness. We are making a thorough change in our lifestyle so that we become agents of happiness. Gradually, we notice that we become kind even in our thoughts. This is a sign that our practice is working at a deep level in us, something to be proud of and thankful for.

In one Greek tradition, the god Hermes laughs the world into existence. Positive humor is indeed a creative act because it pulls back the curtain from a drab human reality and showcases the joy that is always here.

I have a sense of humor, but not at the expense of others. I do not laugh at people's mistakes, distresses, or misfortunes. I feel compassion and look for ways to be supportive. I am less and less apt to engage in ridicule or sarcasm. I forgo using comebacks when others are sarcastic toward me. I seek simply to feel the pain in both of us and look for ways to bring more mutual respect into our communication.

24

Critics No More

IT IS NATURAL for us to assess people and their behavior. Intelligent discernment is a skill of our healthy ego. It can be distinguished from pejorative judgment, which happens when we censure, blame, or look down on others. That tendency is something we can work on through mindfulness and loving-kindness. Here is an example: We have a friend who, we believe, is overly controlling in his behavior toward us. We are mindful as we keep coming back to the pure reality of his behavior but free of our habitual inclinations to condemn or criticize.

We then open ourselves to compassion by practicing a style of loving-kindness. We recognize controlling behavior as a compulsion, a misunderstanding of power, a fear of spontaneity. We say, "May he let go of controlling and thereby find his true spiritual powers. May I not judge others but assess and bless. May all people find this path of freedom from fear."

We can further work on our tendency toward censorious judgment by becoming aware of three common dangers in communication: *criticizing* others, *interfering* in their affairs, giving *advice* that is not specifically requested of us (I call this the "CIA"). This applies especially to how we relate to our family members and our partner. We imagine that we are being of help, but it may be that we rush to these CIA responses because we are not yet comfortable with simply being with others in their predicaments and feelings. Our practice can be to remain present to those who tell us their problems, with no attempts to fix or intervene but with kindly openness to their quandary and the feelings that surround it.

We are mindfully and lovingly present when we manifest the five A's in our listening style: attention, acceptance, appreciation, affection, and allowing someone the space to have his own feelings in his own time and way. The five A's are indeed the tools and antidotes by which we can free ourselves from the knee-jerk CIA style of criticizing, interfering, and advising.

We might at first feel afraid that we are not doing much good when we simply sit and listen with the five A's, but this is how we become really present to others. Such presence creates an intimate atmosphere, a safe and secure container for someone's pain, a mutual trust—the ingredients of healing and bonding. Have we been engaging in the CIA approach because we fear such intimacy? In the face of such a fear we have a program we can turn to, the Triple A technique described in the Introduction. We feel stronger just knowing there are trusty tools that help us handle our stresses; we feel brave because we are willing to use them no matter how daunting our fear may seem.

———————

I look at other people and their choices with discernment but without censure. I still notice the shortcomings of others and of myself, but now I see them as facts to deal with rather than flaws to be condemned in others or in myself. I avoid criticizing, interfering, or giving advice that is not specifically asked for. I avoid those who use this CIA approach toward me, while nonetheless holding them in my spiritual circle of loving-kindness.

———————

PART FIVE

Advancing in the Art of Intimacy

25

The Five A's of Intimacy

INTIMACY BETWEEN two people means showing love to each other without fear or reservations. We can move in this direction by giving and receiving the five A's: *attention* to our partner's needs and feelings, *acceptance* of our partner as she is, *appreciation* expressed regularly and often, *affection* shown in physical ways, and *allowing* our partner the space and encouragement to live out his own calling while asking him to honor the boundaries of the relationship.

Three key practices that help intimacy to grow are as follows:

1. Honoring one another's equal status

2. Keeping agreements

3. Remaining faithful

When we live from a place of loving-kindness and integrity, we are no longer so afraid of being engulfed if our partner gets close nor of feeling abandoned if she is not fully present at times. We do not make unilateral or secret decisions about our relationship. We practice effective and kindhearted communication. We have made an unconditional promise, preferably verbally to our partner, that no matter what he may do, we will never choose the path of retaliation.

We put energy into working through problems by a three-part program, free of blame or defensiveness: We address our issue directly rather than sweep it under the rug. We are willing to process our problem by sharing our feelings and by noticing how our own present predicament may resemble our past, especially our childhood. Finally, we make an agreement to change something so that the immediate problem can be resolved. This leads to letting go of it so that it does not fuel resentments later. Our new agreement is meant to make our future interactions less stressful and more enjoyable.

Despite our best efforts, we or our partner may choose to end the relationship. At the ending of a relationship we remain available to work in therapy if that is appropriate. Our partnerships are conditional; our loving intent is unconditional. So we show integrity and loving-kindness in the process of separating, no matter how our partner behaves toward us.

If equal affection cannot be,
Let the more loving one be me.

    —W. H. AUDEN, "The More Loving One"

In intimate relating, I show and am open to receiving attention, acceptance, appreciation, affection, and allowing. I am committed to working through conflicts by addressing, processing, and resolving them, with help if necessary. If my relationship ends, I act with integrity and loving-kindness and without retaliation.

26

Our Mindsets

IT IS NATURAL for our minds to gravitate toward fear, desire, judgment, control, or illusion. These are all common mindsets in daily life. When they become fixated on our partner, or on ourselves, they can interfere with free-flowing intimacy. Our practice is to take advantage of their positive features and to forgo indulging in them when they sabotage our relationships:

Fear is useful as a signal of threat or danger. When we fear closeness but want relationship, our practice can be the Triple A approach explained earlier: We admit to the other how afraid we feel. We feel our fear fully. We let ourselves experience closeness little by little and more and more, noticing that it *can* feel safe and satisfying too.

Desire is important as a driving force in fulfilling our goals and in reaching out to the one we love. When our desire becomes addictive—insatiable and demanding—it puts pressure on us and on the other person and stresses the relationship. Our goal is to let go of clinging in favor of a tranquil connection to a partner. This will take a willingness to look at the issues, especially those of childhood, that led to such neediness in us. Our practice is addressing, processing, and resolving.

Judgment is healthy as an assessment of what works or does not work in our life and relationships. It becomes deleterious to intimacy when it turns into criticism and censure, both of the other and of ourselves. Our practice then is to see the good in ourselves and others, to let go of blaming, to forgive, and to ask for change but not demand it.

Control is useful in figuring out how to take charge when necessary and how to handle life situations with competence and follow-through. When we try to control others, however, we fail in allowing them to live in accord with their own choices. We work on this by letting go of our ego's need to dominate and by showing respect for the freedom of others.

Illusion works positively when it serves our creative imagination and helps us dream dreams. It becomes an impediment to intimacy when we project beliefs onto someone based on our own expectations, projections, or transferences. Our work then is to realign ourselves to reality by our unconditional yes to the givens of who and how people are.

When certain mindsets interfere with my relating authentically and intimately, I work on letting them go. I want to choose love over fear, contentment with what I have over a needy desire for more, allowing over controlling, acceptance over judgment, and reality over illusion. This is how I become personally clearer in my decisions and ready for real love and intimacy.

27

Mutuality over Competitiveness

HEALTHY COMPETITION helps us hone our skills and
fulfill our potential. Competition becomes negative when
it turns cutthroat. We can look for ways to act in accord
with a collaborative model instead of a dominance model.
We will not choose to participate in business enterprises
that ensure a profit for us while impoverishing others.
Even in sports, we are interested in how the other players
can play better, not only in how we can win. In all of life
we want everyone to win in some way.

In relationships of any kind, people respond to us more
affectionately when we show ourselves to be cooperative.
Competitiveness can be a way of avoiding that intimacy.
Competitiveness in intimate bonds fortifies our ego rather
than the relationship. The practice of cooperation con-
sists of looking for ways to join with others rather than to
contend with them. We want both sides in a conflict to

feel heard and both sides to gain. Such mutuality also includes not pitting one friend or partner against another.

The dominator model and the partnership model are two styles of relating. The dominator model is motivated by control and is based on maintaining the division between superior and inferior. The focus is on hierarchy for the purpose of subjugation and repression of freedom. The partnership model is motivated by the goal of mutual self-actualization through a sharing of power. The focus is on interconnectedness for the purpose of closeness.

Most relationships move back and forth from one model to the other. A choice for intimacy will require careful and caring vigilance over our actions in relationships. Each partner can audit his or her behavior often to see if it has become manipulative and domineering or passive and submissive. Both those extremes sabotage adult interactions.

In healthy relating to a partner, we have given up self-centeredness. Our focus is not on how we can be first but on how both of us can arrive where we want to be, together. We are always looking out for each other. We keep finding ways to assist each other, hand-in-hand, on our common human journey toward mutuality in respect and love.

"Everybody has won and all must have prizes."

—LEWIS CARROLL, *Alice in Wonderland*

I am less and less competitive in relationships and find an uplifting joy in cooperation and community. I believe healthy competition increases my skills, but I shun situations in which my winning means that others have to lose in a demeaning way. My goal is not domination but partnership.

28

Letting Go of Ego

REACTING DEFENSIVELY is a trait of the ego when it is frightened of losing primacy or control. Such defensiveness is a major obstacle to authentic intimacy. Letting go of ego means discarding any arrogant belief in our own entitlement. We begin to see through all the subtle schemes we use so that we can take center stage, get our piece of the pie (no matter who else starves), be right every time, make sure others pay for daring to hurt, cross, or get ahead of us. We can dismantle all those theatrical stage sets of ego so that our healthy ego comes to the fore.

The neurotic ego is the FACE we want so much to save: *fear* of not being liked and acknowledged, *attachment* to being right, *control* of others and of situations, *entitlement* to be loved and respected by everyone with no reciprocal obligation. These are all compulsions that, sadly, become forms of pain for us and for those who have to deal with us.

When people or events upset us, we can look ourselves in the FACE to see precisely how our ego has been aroused. Then we can gently guide our ego to healthier responses: Fear can yield to love, attachment to letting go, control to allowing, entitlement to standing up for ourselves while accepting that our rights are not unconditional and un-limited. Here is the model:

- When I am afraid, I look for a way to be loving.

- When I am attached, I let go.

- When I am trying to control people, I learn to honor their freedom.

- When I feel entitled, I stand up for my reasonable rights and I don't retaliate if I can't secure them.

As we reduce our inflated ego (which is what it truly wanted all along), our healthy ego gains prominence in our life and choices:

- We have a wiser and wider perspective because we are not blinded by the need for immediate gratification. *In relationships this helps us notice the other person's needs.*

- We are no longer driven by greed or self-centeredness, so we become more serene and open. *In relationships this helps us be less competitive and more cooperative.*

- We manage our own needs better. *In relationships we are not so demanding and dependent on others.*

- We gain equanimity in conflicts and calamities because we have let go of the compulsion to be in full control. *In relationships this helps us calmly address, process, and resolve our problems.*

I know I can never give up on my labor of love: to keep winning my ego back from its misguided tendency to inflate, defend, and highlight itself and thereby lose its chance to find the love it so desperately craves—but so often fears.

29

Healthy Sexuality

IN HIS BOOK *Love and Living,* the Christian contemplative Thomas Merton defined purity in a way that delightfully transcends the usual definitions: "It is precisely in the spirit of celebration, gratitude, and joy that true purity is found."

It is an adult spiritual practice to honor our sexuality by balancing enjoyment and responsibility. This may mean taking a careful inventory of our sexual behavior:

- Does our sexual style include exploiting or taking advantage of others?

- Are we using sex as a weapon or in other manipulative ways?

- Is our authentic sexual orientation hidden?

- Has our sexual style become addictive? If so, we seek help from a twelve-step program.

It's worthwhile to explore the elements in our sexuality that may still be held hostage by puritanical beliefs and taboos meant to scare and restrict us rather than liberate us. For instance, we may believe that it is wrong to seek sexual pleasure as an end in itself or that harmless erotic fantasy or certain behaviors among adults are verboten if they extend beyond conventional limits.

We may also wonder how our sexuality meshes with our spirituality. This link becomes visible when we let go of attachment to such dualisms as freedom versus obligation, male versus female, human versus divine. These sharp divisions can begin to blur in favor of integration. We find that we more readily let our whole bodymind fit into our spirituality. We can bring consciousness of our sexuality into our most sacred moments and consciousness of the divine into our most earthy experiences. The mystic poet William Blake wrote, "The Lamb of God sports in the gardens of sexual delight."

Finally, we may feel frustrated or believe something is wrong with us because we are doubtful or unhappy about our sexual desires, performance, or level of satisfaction in sex. In that regard we can be kinder to ourselves. No one is expected to integrate fully or for a lifetime the following three human conundrums: sex, food, money. At best, we make friends peaceably with each of these three imps here and there, now and then. Can we love ourselves enough to let that be all right with us? Can we let go of the need to be perfect? Can we be satisfied with a beginner's mind? Can we live with the ragged edges and uncertain innuendoes that keep life so immensely energizing?

I want my sexual style to adhere to the same standards of integrity and loving-kindness that apply in all areas of my life. More and more, my sexuality expresses love, joyful playfulness, and responsibility. I am letting go of inappropriate guilt or phobia in favor of the liberty of relating and enjoying. This opens me to the spiritual dimensions of sexuality.

30

Trust and Trustworthiness

WE TRUST OTHERS when the long-term record shows they have been consistently trustworthy or have made amends for the times when they were not. We trust others when they keep coming through for us, show sincere caring for us, and rejoice in our successes. We trust others when we see their genuineness: the same person inside as outside, the words and behavior matching. We show our trustworthiness toward others in those same ways.

Our adult trust is conditional, but our trustworthiness can be unconditional: Our trust in others is conditional because uncertainty is a given of life, so trusting will always be an act of daring. Yet we can act in trustworthy ways toward others, because that has become our standard and our practice.

This trust model—conditionality in our responses to others and unconditionality in our way of acting toward others—can be a model for all our interactions: We may not always be treated kindly, but we are kind nonetheless. We may not always be thanked, but we show gratitude nonetheless. We may not always be shown generosity, but we are generous nonetheless.

This practice of "nonetheless" is a path to freedom since we are no longer caught in a chain reaction with others that directs how we act or react. We can choose the standard of love no matter what others may do. We then notice ourselves becoming more flexible, less controlling, more understanding, accepting others just as they are—sometimes loyal and kind, sometimes disloyal and unkind. In fact, the unkindness of others can trigger more kindness on our part. We know how hurt we feel and we don't want anyone else to feel that way.

Trusting ourselves is the foundation for all other forms of trust. How do we develop trust in ourselves?

- We are consistently self-nurturant.

- We absent ourselves from those who show they intend to keep hurting, betraying, or lying to us.

- We make the transition from fantasy and projection to concrete realism about ourselves, others, and events.

- We count on ourselves gladly to receive the trustworthiness of a partner with appreciation and sadly to handle betrayal without retaliation.

- We are open to rebuilding trust when it has been broken. This takes mutual willingness to work things out and time to see that a new record is in place. We are able to forgive while remaining intelligently cautious since we are familiar with the checkered history of all us humans. This is how our yes to the givens of human behavior can combine self-nurturance with healthy relating.

I am learning to trust others when the record shows they can be trusted, while I, nonetheless, commit myself to being trustworthy no matter what others may do. I am always open to rebuilding trust when it has been broken.

PART SIX

Reaching Out Beyond Ourselves

31

Confronted with a Suffering World

WE CAN BE TOUCHED by the suffering not only of our loved ones but also of people in the wider world. This is how we loosen our narrow boundaries so that our love can become universal. In great compassion, our caring about suffering is automatically a choice to relieve it. Our answer to the question, why is there suffering? is not theoretical. It becomes a practice: What can I do to heal it?

Compassion does not have to be from the top down. We can transcend the attitude of "helping those less fortunate than ourselves." We show compassion because we are involved so intimately with all humanity that we see ourselves as part of their suffering, either as complicit in how it happened or as a fellow human on life's sometimes painful path.

Our compassion is not limited to responding to people who are downtrodden. It also takes the form of dissent and protest against the agencies and policies that create the conditions of suffering. Martin Luther King Jr. once said, "Compassion is more than flinging a coin to a beggar; it understands that an edifice which produces beggars needs restructuring." Our voices and boycotts can be aimed at the vast military-corporate alliances that produce nuclear weaponry, use up or hoard planetary resources, and generate injustice and inequality the world over—the alarming symptoms of collective decadence. We can take our stand for an economic system that serves rather than exploits our ecosystem.

This level of spiritual awareness includes a letting go of excessive partisanship. We support a political party, but we want the current president to do the best job he or she can for all of us rather than hoping for failure so that our party candidate can succeed next term. This is a genuine caring for the commonweal, beyond partisan or bipartisan to trans-partisan.

We do not have to hate those who hurt the world; we can try to win them over. We can trust in the possibility of transformation of every political and religious leader and policy: As Martin Luther King Jr. said, "I have a dream that one day this nation will rise up and live out the true meaning of its creed . . . that all men are created equal." Such hope follows from our belief in goodness— ever alive in all of us, even in those corrupted by power.

Confronted with the suffering in the world, I do not turn my eyes away nor do I get stuck in blaming God or humanity, but simply ask, "What, then, shall I do?" I do what I can to relieve suffering and to take a stand against policies that cause it. My belief in the goodness in all of us is helping me work for the transformation of those responsible for injustice. I offer time, attention, money, myself, no matter how minimal the result. As the saying goes, "It is better to light one candle than to curse the darkness."

32

Dedication to Nonviolence

IF WE ARE COMMITTED to manifesting loving-kindness, we should support policies of nonviolence in world affairs. This is consistent with our aspiration to be assertive rather than aggressive or abusive. Buddhist scholar Robert Thurman writes, "If one sincerely upholds the truth, its simple power will eventually overwhelm injustice." If we believe that, we won't give up, be afraid to take a stand, or believe that our individual efforts make no difference. We will trust in the power of our single voice to contribute to the building of a critical mass of peace workers so that a change can happen in world politics.

We cannot deny our collective human tendency toward violence, which is shown in greed, retaliation, war, genocide, torture, hate crimes. We know there will always be violence of some kind in this rough-and-tumble world.

Our inherent goodness sits beside our inherent inclination toward aggression.

Yet we trust that good can triumph: We reckon evil as real but not primary or final. We notice that there are always hands raised in protest against violence and in cheers for the ways of peace. We ourselves never give up on the possibility of more love on the world stage. *There will never be only love or only peace, but there can be more love than before we got here and more peace because we were here.*

We are also conscious of violence toward nature. Our commitment to cherish and preserve nature—as stewards, not owners—means that we do not destroy, nor do we support companies that exploit natural habitats for the sake of monetary gain. We do not invest in companies that cause harm to the environment.

Our goal is also to work toward a society in which lawbreakers make restitution, contribute to the community, are rehabilitated, and see the light. This is restorative rather than retributive justice. When our concept of rebalancing an injustice changes in this way, it is not simply finding a new definition of justice, it is a sign that a spiritual transformation has happened in us.

We may design a spiritual practice for watching or listening to the news, such as the following: we do not simply watch a segment about the horrors that happen daily, we let ourselves feel grief and compassion. Then the news is spiritually interactive because we feel sad, angry, and afraid because of the losses and the terrors. We also show our compassion for the suffering by our loving-kindness practice, prayer, or aspiration in the moment of our hearing the news: "May we all work nonviolently to put an end to war and injustice."

I am committing myself to fighting injustice in nonviolent ways. I support restorative rather than retributive justice. I am distressed and feel myself called to action by the disasters of genocide, nuclear armaments, economic injustice, racial oppression, pollution, and violations of human rights. I keep thinking globally and acting locally in any way I can.

33

Living with Purpose

MOST OF US HAVE had a variety of purposes and goals in our lives. They have been based both on opportunities that have come our way and on our inner drives and dreams. When we commit ourselves to loving-kindness, our purposes seem to align with our unique talents, what makes us happy, what seems to fulfill us, and what contributes to the benefit of others.

We might also wonder if life has an overall purpose, one that is shared by the collective of humanity. One way to explore that question is to notice that the universe does seem to have an inner directedness. That direction reveals itself in those evolutionary moments when the world moves toward more consciousness and more connectedness. Our larger-than-individual-life purpose can perhaps be found when consciousness blooms in us as wisdom, and connectedness as an expression of love.

When that happens in us, we may feel assured that nature is zealously working out its purpose *in and through us*. We increase our cooperation by seeking ever more respectful ways of surviving with our planet instead of on it. Indeed, the philosopher and Jesuit priest Pierre Teilhard de Chardin chose "to pray with all the elements and with matter itself, to draw strength from the enduring powers of nature, and to overcome the forces of alienation that threaten to depersonalize modern culture."

We can explore how purposefully we are living our life, both on the individual and on the collective level, by looking deeply into our work, projects, relationships, and memberships in groups. Do they nourish our consciousness and connectedness? We can ask questions like these and make any life change, however small, that helps us answer affirmatively to the following:

- Is this relationship or group helping me widen my vision of my place in the world so that I see beyond my own immediate needs?

- Is my sense of connection expanding from those near and dear to those far and wide?

- Am I being challenged and supported to move from greed to generosity, from hatred to compassion, from illusion to realism, from narrowness to universality?

- Is my consciousness of the ecology growing in such a way that I now practice what Saint Bonaventure recommends: "a courtesy toward natural things"?

- Is my lifestyle in keeping with my deepest needs, values, and wishes while, at the same time, contributing to those of the planet?

I ask this question as I embark upon any relationship or career choice: Is this a suitable context in which I can fulfill my life purpose to grow in wisdom and love, to share my personal gifts, and to cocreate a peaceful future for our planet?

34

Not Giving Up on Others

OUR CAPACITY TO LOVE and to believe in lovability is not extinguished, nor does it have to be diminished by what others do. For instance, as we grow in compassion we begin to interpret the behavior of those people who come at us aggressively as their sadly confused way of making a connection or as an expression of their own pain. They are letting us know they need love but don't know how to ask for it. Imagine how loving we will become as we begin to interpret all forms of communication to us as direct, indirect, or misdirected pleas for love.

We do not have to give up on others—no matter how they behave. We can affirm that human goodness is primary and ineradicable in ourselves and in others. This is an operative faith in inherent goodness, a feature of what is variously called "buddha nature," "Christ consciousness," or "the inner light of every human being." Such faith is not a denial of our negative capabilities or our shadow side but an affirmation of our inborn potential to let love now, soon, and finally take invincible precedence in our daily decisions.

The best practice for becoming aware of the goodness in everyone is to show our own goodness by acts of love. This is stated well by the Spanish mystic Saint John of the Cross: "Where there is no love, show love, and then you will find it." We can thereby grow in trust that our love has such power that, even from afar, it can evoke and activate the intrinsic goodness that is in others.

Each of us shows love in a signature way, unique to us but readable by anyone. Our love can take specific forms: We may offer others one or more of the five A's: attention, acceptance, appreciation, affection, and allowing. Or we may specialize our style of loving by our unique brand of sensitivity and caring.

We can cherish the artful signature of love that is already ours. We can also be on the lookout for ever new ways of actualizing our full capacity for loving so that more and more people benefit. This does not mean losing our boundaries carelessly but opening our hearts fearlessly. Every commitment in this book is meant to get us there. The following daily, anytime aspiration—one that pulls out all the stops—may also help. It may appeal to us as a courageous declaration, an irrepressible affirmation of our life purpose, why we are here, what we were meant for, what we are really about:

May I show all the love I have
In any way I can
Here, now, and all the time,
To everything and everyone—including me—
Since love is what we are—and why.
Now nothing matters to me more
Or gives me greater joy.

I am trusting more and more that everyone has an innate goodness and that being loved by someone can release it. I want to be that someone.

35

Cosmic Religion, Cosmic Spirituality

RELIGION AND SPIRITUALITY can be resources for transformation. Both have the same four components: beliefs, moral standards, rituals, and devotion. In a religion, these four occur in a group or institution with a common creed, a specific moral code, official rituals, and prescribed forms of devotion. In spirituality the four elements are designed by the individual and practiced in his or her own way, since the authority to evaluate is within. The dramatic and gripping elements of religion can then be reframed in a personal spirituality.

The danger in an institution is that it can become controlling and parochial. The danger in a strictly private spirituality is that it can be about what's comfortable for us and not include the challenges we need to grow, especially the social ones. Religion and spirituality can, of course, be combined in one's life and choices when each of the four components of religion and spirituality become cosmic in scope and growth-promoting.

Belief based on the word of authority figures, rather than one's own experience, can be constricting. Beliefs that are taken literally can limit us to a childish level of understanding. In cosmic-wide consciousness, we recognize religious stories as metaphors for our mysterious journey as a planetary community. Rather than regarding everything dualistically—good versus bad, right versus wrong—we see the divine in all that is.

Morality can focus mostly on our own personal virtues and failings. However, in a cosmic view, our conscience is attuned to the social inequalities and abuses that we directly or indirectly support. Our moral sense then expands to include caring for the needs of the world.

Rituals are often considered valid or meaningful only if they follow traditional forms. Yet, we can design our own rituals that are more in keeping with contemporary themes, even while continuing to derive meaning from age-old, universal archetypes.

Devotion includes feelings and the forming of a personal relationship to a God or indwelling Spirit. This can take the form of reverence for nature. We can also show devotedness to figures, living or dead, whom we admire for their expansive love and whom we choose to imitate.

The ancient Jewish historian, Flavius Josephus, wrote in *Contra Apionem*: "I suppose it will become evident [someday] that the laws in the Torah are meant to lead to a universal love of humanity." Our challenge as universal humans is to dedicate ourselves to building a world of justice, peace, and love. In fact, our commitment to integrity and loving-kindness is just what is required if we are not to become an endangered species. W. H. Auden, in his poem "September 1, 1939," stated our final options well: "We must love one another or die."

I am widening my beliefs, my moral standards, my choice of rituals, and my devotion in ever more inclusive ways. Both religion and spirituality are available to me as resources.

36

Appreciation for Grace

IN HIS BOOK *Nine Talmudic Readings*, the French philosopher Emmanuel Levinas presents a paradox: "What is truly human is beyond human strength." In other words, we can put great effort into our commitments to transforming ourselves and our world, but only the free gift of grace can evoke the shifts that make the final difference. This can be felt as a divine concurrence in or boost to our efforts. Grace is how we describe the assisting force of wisdom and courage beyond our ordinary powers that keeps wonderfully coming to us on our life journey. Grace is accessible always, everywhere, to everyone since it is not only around us but deep within us. All that is required of us is openness.

The self-help movement sometimes proclaims that we create our own reality. This can give the shaming impression that we are to blame for our circumstances. It can also deteriorate into the illusion that we are in full control.

Such a belief overlooks the power of unconscious forces, especially those in dreams, synchronicity, the shadow, divine inspiration and powers—manifold ways that grace comes through to us.

As we advance in spiritual awareness, we pay attention to all these forces in and around us. Then we more clearly behold the vast array of our spiritual resources and guides and we look for ways to accept their generous help. Carl Jung wrote, "Attention to the unconscious pays it a compliment that guarantees its cooperation."

In this last chapter we can acknowledge the grace of finding practices of integrity and loving-kindness. Since grace is not based on merit, we do not consider ourselves above other people because we are choosing to practice the commitments in this book. We do not judge others for not following them. We do not demand that others adhere to them. Indeed, there is no elitism in authentic spirituality. As Lin-chi, the Chinese Buddhist teacher, said, "Enlightenment means having no rank."

Our practice is to be thankful, first of all, for our most fundamental and significant grace, our innate and inalienable goodness. Our gratitude then opens us to a warm caring for others in three world-evolving ways: trust, hope, and loyalty.

- We *trust* that everyone has goodness and that it will appear in them when the time is right, just as it did and does for us.

- We actively *hope* that others find the joy we are finding in our enduring commitment to integrity and loving-kindness.

- We always remain *loyal* to those forlorn in the ever-darkening dusk of fear and discontent.

Our caring in these ways shows how grace is complete when what we receive is also what we give.

I see whatever love and wisdom I may have as gifts, spiritual energies that come not from me but through me. I say thanks for these encouraging graces and yes to the stirring call to live up to them. I keep looking for ways to share my blessings, not as one who is above others but as one who stands beside them.

Conclusion

Our Full-Size Destiny

We cannot rest until everyone mirrors the divinity in
everything.

—HERMANN GRAF KEYSERLING

WE FULFILL OURSELVES only by surpassing ourselves.
Our challenge is to seek more than our own individual
progress toward integrity and loving-kindness. We want
to see these evolving in everyone; we want to do all we
can to help that happen.

This is not too much to ask of ourselves. Our goals
could never have been only personal since our psyches

are not only personal. We have a collective consciousness that makes us responsive to world myths, and our dreams are certainly full of universal symbols. We are connected to one another genetically and historically. Our individual bodies are cells in the one mystical body of the universe.

Our personal gifts have only to be opened into their fullest emergent possibility, that of cocreating a brighter and kinder world. This will take thinking big, a radical expansion of our imagination and our optimism. It will mean taking on a four-part challenge: trust, vision, practice, outreach:

- We will have to *trust* that an embrace of honest and loving ways of living can indeed happen not only in individuals but in corporations, institutions, schools, churches, and nations.

- We can *envision* the commitments in this book taking hold in the wider world. When we fervently and continuously picture a world of uprightness and caring, we form an intention that can help it happen.

- We continue *practicing* our commitments in our own relationships, jobs, political affiliations, religious communities, and society. When others see our joy in living out our commitments, they will want it too. Ultimately, we do not convince others by preaching or proselytizing but by example.

- We look for ways to *reach out* to others and to interest them in making the commitments that have now become important to us. We bring up the topic of integrity and loving-kindness with individuals or groups. We initiate a discussion and share our personal experience, if others are open to that. We may use the list of commitments in the appendix of this book to encourage sharing and discussing.

The spiritual power of grace will find ways to help us. Perhaps Pierre Teilhard de Chardin referred to this when he wrote, "So long as our being is tensed passionately into the spirit in everything, then that spirit will emerge from our hidden, nameless efforts."

The future we work toward is nothing less than a world in which integrity and loving-kindness become universal standards. That will be a world of justice, peace, equality, liberty, and love—our best way to begin and the only way for us not to end.

We see all this as possible because we can dream and build on dreams. To build a new world is what we are here for and what we are capable of. All it takes is not being afraid of or in doubt about the enduring power of our basic goodness and its irrepressible zeal to display itself in innumerable ways.

Our calling is, of course, not single-handedly to end the aggression and injustice in our society but to join together with the many people in the world right now whose energetic voices and hands are working toward that goal. Perhaps one more heart with optimism—ours—will tip the scales into the specific density of commitment that is required for world change. *Wasn't our birth certificate a promissory note for that?*

It all happens when we trust that we, you and I, are present, right here and now, at the birth of a new humanity in, from, and for our long-waiting world.

Appendix

Our Commitments to Loving-Kindness

Use the following list as a summary and a reminder of the main commitments to loving-kindness discussed in this book. You are welcome to copy and share it. It can spur discussion—and enthusiasm—in any group, family, classroom, or relationship. A list of similar commitments can also be downloaded from the free section of my Web site, www.davericho.com.

- I do my best to keep my word, honor commitments, and follow through on the tasks I have agreed to do.

- I am making every attempt to abide by standards of rigorous honesty, truthfulness, and respect in all my dealings no matter how others act toward me.

- I forgo taking advantage of anyone because of his or her ignorance, misfortune, or financial straits. My question is not "What can I get away with?" but "What is the right thing to do?" If I fall down in this, I can admit it, make amends, and resolve to act differently the next time. Now I more easily and willingly apologize when necessary.

- If someone is overly generous toward me or has an exaggerated sense of obligation to me, I do not want to exploit his or her lack of boundaries. Instead, I express appreciation and work out an equitable way of interacting.

- I keep examining my conscience with true candor. I am taking searching inventories, not only about how I may have harmed others, but also about how I may not have activated my potentials or shared my gifts, how I may still be holding on to prejudices or the will to retaliate, and how I may still not be as loving, inclusive, and open as I can be.

- I welcome feedback that shows me where I am less caring than I could be, where I am less tolerant, and less open about my real feelings. When I am shown that I've been mean or inauthentic, I am not defensive but take it as information about what I have to work on. I appreciate positive feedback also.

- I am letting go of the need to keep up appearances or to project an overly impressive self-image. I now want to appear as I am, without pretense and no matter how unflattering.

- I do not want to use any charms of body, word, or mind to trick or seduce others. Being loved for who I am has become more important—and more interesting—than upholding the ever-shaky status of my ego.

- I now measure my success by how much steadfast love I have, not by how much I have in the bank, how much I achieve in business, or how much power I have over others. The central—and most exhilarating—focus of my life is to show all my love in the style uniquely mine, in every way I can, here and now, always and everywhere, no one excluded.

- As I say yes to the reality of who I am, with pride in my gifts and unabashed awareness of my limits, I notice I can love myself and that I become more lovable too.

- I never give up on believing that everyone has an innate goodness and that being loved can evoke it.

- I am learning to trust others when the record shows they can be trusted while I, nonetheless, commit myself to being trustworthy no matter what others may do. I am always open to rebuilding trust when it has been broken, if the other is willing.

- I am willing to participate in the harmless conventions and social rituals that make others happy.

- I am learning to ask for what I need without demand, manipulation, or expectation. As I honor the timing, wishes, and limits of others, I can show respect by taking no for an answer.

- I do not knowingly hurt or intend to offend others. I act kindly toward others, not to impress or obligate them, but because I really am kind—or working on it. If others fail to thank me or to return my kindness, that does not have to stop me from behaving lovingly nonetheless.

- If people hurt me, I can say, "Ouch!" and ask to open a dialogue. I may ask for amends, but I can drop the topic if they are not forthcoming. No matter what, I do not choose to retaliate, hold grudges, keep a record of wrongs, or hate anyone. "What goes around comes around" has become "May what goes around come around *transformatively*." This also means that I do not gloat over the sufferings or defeats of those who have hurt me.

- I do not let others abuse me, but I interpret their harshness as coming from their own pain and as a sadly confused way of letting me know they need connection but don't know how to ask for it in healthy ways. I recognize this with concern, not with censure or scorn.

- I remain open to reconciling with others after conflict. At the same time, I am learning to release those who show themselves to be unwilling to relate to me respectfully. I accept the given of sudden unexplained silence or rejection by others and will never use that style myself.

- I am practicing ways to show my anger against unfairness directly and nonviolently rather than in abusive, threatening, blaming, out-of-control, or passive ways.

- I have a sense of humor but not at the expense of others. I want to use humor to poke fun at human foibles, especially my own. I do not engage in ridicule, put-downs, taunting, teasing, sarcasm, or "comebacks." When others use hurtful humor toward me, I want to feel the pain in both of us and look for ways to bring more mutual respect into our communication.

- I do not laugh at people or their mistakes, distresses, or misfortunes but look for ways to be supportive.

- I notice how in some groups there are people who are humiliated or excluded. Rather than be comforted that I am still safely an insider, especially by gossiping about them, I want to sense the pain in being an outsider. Then I can reach out and include everyone in my circle of love, compassion, and respect.

- I look at other people and their choices with intelligent discernment but without censure. I still notice the shortcomings of others and of myself, but now I am beginning to see them as facts to deal with rather than flaws to be criticized or be ashamed of. Accepting others as they are has become more important to me than whether they are what I want them to be.

- I avoid Criticizing, Interfering, or giving Advice that is not specifically asked for. I take care of myself by staying away from those who use this CIA approach toward me, while nonetheless holding them in my spiritual circle of loving-kindness. Accepting others as they are has become more important to me than whether they are what I want them to be.

- I am less and less competitive in relationships at home and work and find happiness in cooperation and community. I shun situations in which my winning means that others lose in a humiliating way.

- In intimate bonds, I honor equality, keep agreements, work on problems, and act in respectful and trustworthy ways. My goal is not to use a relationship to gratify my ego but to dispossess myself of ego to gratify the relationship. Also, I respect the boundaries of others' relationships.

- I want my sexual style to adhere to the same standards of integrity and loving-kindness that apply in all areas of my life. More and more, my sexuality expresses love, passion, and joyful playfulness. I remain committed to a responsible, adult style of relating and enjoying.

- Confronted with the suffering in the world, I do not turn my eyes away, nor do I get stuck in blaming God or humanity but simply ask, "What, then, shall I do?" I keep finding ways to respond even if it has to be minimal: "It is better to light one candle than to curse the darkness."

- I appreciate that whatever love or wisdom I may have or show comes not from me but through me. I say thanks for these encouraging graces and yes to the stirring call to live up to them.

- I am not hard on myself when I fail to live up to these ideals. I just keep earnestly practicing. The sincerity of my intention and my ongoing efforts are the measure of my success.

- I do not think I am above other people because I honor this list. I do not demand that others follow it.

- I am sharing this list with those who are open to it and I keep believing that someday these commitments can become the style not only of individuals but of corporations, institutions, churches, and nations.

About the Author

DAVID RICHO, PHD, MFT, is a psychotherapist and workshop leader who lives in Santa Barbara and San Francisco, California. He combines Jungian, Buddhist, and mythic perspectives in his work. He is the author of numerous books on psychological and spiritual growth. For more information, including upcoming events and a catalog of audio and video programs, visit www.davericho .com.

Also by David Richo

Shadow Dance: Liberating the Power and Creativity of Your Dark Side (Shambhala, 1999)

The shadow is all that we abhor about ourselves and all the dazzling potential that we doubt or deny we have. We project these onto others as dislike or admiration. We can restore these capacities to ourselves. Our dark side then becomes a source of creativity and awakens our untapped potential.

How to Be An Adult in Relationships: The Five Keys to Mindful Loving (Shambhala, 2002)

Love is not so much a feeling as a way of being present. Love is presence with these five A's: unconditional attention, acceptance, appreciation, affection, and allowing others to be as they are. Love is also a way of being present without the five conditioned overlays of ego: judgment, fear, control, attachment, and illusion.

The Five Things We Cannot Change and the Happiness
We Find by Embracing Them (Shambhala, 2005)
There are unavoidable "givens" in life and relationships.
By our unconditional yes to these conditions of existence
we learn to open, accept, and even embrace our predicaments without trying to control the outcomes. We begin
to trust what happens in our lives as gifts of grace that
help us grow in character, depth, and compassion.

The Power of Coincidence: How Life Shows Us
What We Need to Know (Shambhala, 2007)
There are meaningful coincidences of events, dreams, or
relationships that happen to us and are beyond our control. These synchronicities influence the course of our life
in mysterious ways. They often reveal assisting forces that
are pointing us to our unguessed, unexpected, and un-
imagined destiny.

The Sacred Heart of the World: Restoring Mystical
Devotion to Our Spiritual Life (Paulist Press, 2007)
We explore the symbolism of the heart in world religious
traditions, and then trace the historical thread of Christian devotion to the Sacred Heart of Jesus into modern
times. We focus on the philosophy and theology of Teilhard de Chardin and Karl Rahner to design a new sense
of what devotion can be.

Mary Within Us: A Jungian Contemplation of Her Titles & Powers (Human Development Books, 2007)

The Jungian archetype of the feminine aspect of God as personified by Mary is built into the design of every human psyche. The ancient titles of Mary are a summary of the qualities of our essential Self. In fact, every religious truth and image is a metaphor for potentials in us and in the universe.

Wisdom's Way: Quotations for Meditation (Human Development Books, 2008)

This is a book of quotations from a variety of sources, especially Buddhist, Christian, Jungian, and transpersonal. The quotations are brief and can be used as springboards for meditation. They are divided into three sections: psychological insight, spiritual awareness, and mystical realization.

Making Love Last: How to Sustain Intimacy and Nurture Connection (Set of 3 CDs, Shambhala, 2008)

This is an audio recording of a lively one-day workshop on relationship issues given by David Richo at Spirit Rock Retreat Center in California. Topics include how love can endure, fears of intimacy and commitment, resolving our conflicts, the phases of a relationship, how our early life affects our adult relationships.

When the Past Is Present: Healing the Emotional Wounds That Sabotage Our Relationships (Shambhala, 2008)
Transference is a tendency to see our parents or other significant characters in our life story in others. We explore how our past impacts our present relationships. We find ways to make transference a valuable opportunity to learn about ourselves, deepen our relationships, and heal our old wounds.

Being True to Life: Poetic Paths to Personal Growth (Shambhala, 2009)
Poetry may have seemed daunting in school but here is a chance for it to become quite wonderfully personal and spiritually enriching. This book offers an opportunity to use our hearts and pens to release the full range of our imagination to discover ourselves through reading and writing poetry.

Daring to Trust: Opening Ourselves to Real Love and Intimacy (Shambhala, 2010)
We learn how to build trust, how to recognize a trustworthy person, how to work with our fears around trusting, and how to rebuild trust after a breach or infidelity. We find ways to trust others, to trust ourselves, to trust reality, what happens to us, and to trust a higher power than ourselves.